THE FOUR HORSEMEN

THE FOUR HORSEMEN

Racism, Sexism, Militarism and Social Darwinism

ETHEL TOBACH
JOHN GIANUTSOS
HOWARD R. TOPOFF
CHARLES G. GROSS

Behavioral Publications
New York

Library of Congress Catalog Number 73-18052
ISBN: 0-87705-121-6
Copyright © 1974 by Behavioral Publications

BEHAVIORAL PUBLICATIONS
72 Fifth Avenue
New York, New York 10011

Printed in the United States of America
456789   987654321

Library of Congress Cataloging in Publication Data
Main entry under title:

The Four horsemen: racism, sexism, militarism, and social Darwinism.

Papers based on a panel discussion at the American Orthopsychiatric
Association 1972 national convention.
1. Aggressiveness (Psychology) 2. Behavior modification. 3. Science—
Social aspects. I. Tobach, Ethel, 1921-   ed. II. American Orthopsychiatric Association. [DNLM: 1. Behavior—Congresses. 2. Psychiatry—Congresses. WM100 F773 1972]
BF575.A3F66   301.4   73-18052

Contents

Authors

John Gianutsos
Adelphi University

C. G. Gross
Princeton University

Ethel Tobach
Department of Animal Behavior
The American Museum of Natural History
New York, New York

Howard Topoff
Department of Psychology
Hunter College of the City University of New York
and
Department of Animal Behavior
The American Museum of Natural History
New York, New York

Acknowledgements

We wish to thank the American Orthopsychiatric Association for initiating an invitation to Psychologists for Social Action to organize a session on a topic of urgent and current interest to the professions which make up their association. The authors of this volume had spoken and written on these topics in the past, but it was the current panel discussion at the American Orthopsychiatric 1972 national convention that brought the four of us together. We hope that this theme will become part of a widespread discussion by all citizens.

Introduction

When the Conference on which this book is based was organized, the prophets of doom were in full sway. We were told that the only way to control racism was to use drugs. We were told that the only way to control instinctive patterns of violence and aggression was through psychosurgery. We were told that the economic welfare of this country was being threatened by a need to support vast populations of individuals whose genetic inferiority made it impossible for them to survive the advanced technological society in which we lived. We were told that to form a more perfect state in which human beings could survive, a system of training and control was needed so that the nonviable concepts of freedom and dignity could be supplanted by concepts that would guarantee the survival of the culture.

There seemed to be a common thread running through all these proposed means of controlling human behavior. The thread was that of impending doom for humanity because of inherent human evil. This brought to mind the apocalyptic metaphor of the four horsemen bringing death, famine, war, and disease. A friend (G. Vroman) gently pointed out that

13

this picture was not accurate, if it were based on the original horsemen and horses as depicted in The Revelation of John in the New Testament. These horses and horsemen were:

> a white horse, and its rider carried a bow. He was given a crown, and rode forth as a victor to conquer . . .
> another horse . . . bright red, and its rider was given power to take peace away from the earth and make men slaughter one another; he was given a great sword . . .
> a black horse, and its rider had a pair of scales in his hand . . . and a voice . . . seemed to come from the midst of the four animals . . . wheat at a dollar a quart, and barley three quarts for a dollar, but you must not injure the oil and wine! . . .
> a livid horse, and its rider's name was Death, and Hades followed him. They were given power over one quarter of the earth, to kill the people with sword, famine, death and the wild animals of the earth.

Neither did the metaphor conform with the four horsemen of the Spanish novelist Vicente Blasco Ibanez or the Hollywood movie starring Rudolf Valentino. With an apology to the history of the metaphor, we propose that we are faced again with the specter of four horsemen. This time, the four horsemen are racism, sexism, militarism, and Social Darwinism. Each of the horsemen represents groups of scientists. One group is made up of traditional ethologists who believe that the evolution and modification of behavior are explainable in terms of inherited genetic mechanisms that determine behavior; these instinc-

tive patterns can be controlled by diversion or training to produce harmless, socially acceptable patterns
of behavior. Another group sees no difference in the
neural organization of human and infra-human organisms and conceives of the control of social behavior through electro-physiological manipulation of
neural functions. A third group envisions control
over the inherited evil of humanity through biochemical means, either through genetic engineering
and eugenic controls or through biochemicals administered in the form of drugs. The fourth group
sees the genetic endowment of populations as the
limiting factor for any possible beneficial modification of behavior. They propose to use engineered
techniques to diagnose the individual's behavior, and
to then control the behavior of the individual
through special training designed to maintain existing class and ethnic relationships. These class and
ethnic relationships are considered timeless and un-
changing in regard to basic human characteristics,
although the forms of the behavior may change. The
freedom and dignity of the individual to make the
choices is considered a scientifically invalid concept.

Not only are the horsemen composites of groups of
individuals, but they also change horses readily, possibly because the concept of inherited behavior patterns is fundamental to all groups. As a result, in
dealing with any one of the four—racism, sexism,
militarism, and Social Darwinism—it is impossible
to restrict oneself to only one group of horsemen.
Thus, there is some overlap in the papers—a reflec-
tion of the unity that exists among the four
horsemen.

We are not proposing that there is, in the scientific community, a John the Baptist who will stand up and call the names of those who are forecasting doom and rally the scientific community to a struggle with the four horsemen. We are proposing instead that the scientific community needs to become consciously aware of the relationship between the scientist and society. The assumptions underlying scientific theory need to be made explicit and then tested. The way in which the data are gathered, how results of such investigations are used, and other aspects of the business of being a scientist need to be discussed by the scientist. Scientists must formulate proposals for the carrying out of these activities in ways which are acceptable not only to the scientific community, but to society as well. Most important, the way in which the assumptions are tested needs to be discussed with all of the individuals involved—the society of nonscientists as well as the society of scientists. This kind of task is difficult for the scientist, but, we believe, eminently feasible and desirable.

Please note that I do not wish to prescribe the value systems to be followed by scientists. I hope that this book will stimulate scientists to view themselves as subject to the same societal processes as other members of society—the same economic pressures, the same social motivations and prejudices. A scientist may be a bigot; be personally exploitative of family, friends, and co-workers; be a supernationalist patriot; believe in war as a solution to international political conflict; or, be an anarchist, pacifist, militant radical, liberal dissenter, or outstanding altruist. These attitudes and behavior patterns may play some role in the choosing of a research problem or theoretical position. The value systems and attitudes of the individual may be more significant in the choice of colleagues, students and assistants. They are likely to be most relevant to the uses to which the scientist is willing to put the results of the work done.

In the last four decades changes in societal structure and in social customs throughout the world have made it difficult for the scientist to ignore such issues. Nonscientific sectors of many societies are confronting the scientific community with a demand for justification of the activities of scientists. Those who support the activities of scientists are demanding that scientists themselves either assume responsibility for what they are doing or submit to control by other means.

If we restrict ourselves to more recent history, the response of the Luddites to technical change, the reaction to the use of atomic energy, and the concern with the depletion of natural resources through overuse and pollution are clear examples of societal demands for the justification of social applications of scientfic research. In the last two instaces, these demands have extended to justification of basic research itself. All the examples cited so far stemmed from research in the physical and chemical sciences.

Today, the development of the many branches of biological and psychological sciences has brought us to analogous situations in those areas of knowledge. Instead of machines that change the physical world and our relationship to it in ways that are not acceptable, we are faced with techniques that may change our bodies in ways that are not acceptable to us: genetic engineering; drugs and surgical intervention; behavioral control through psychological techniques; and selective breeding programs that might preclude the survival of whole groups of people.

Scientists have always been controlled by some group or other in the nonscientific community. They have fought for the right to pursue their inquiries regardless of the resulting challenges to society. They have never fought as vigorously for the understanding and implementation of their responsibilities to the rest of society. They may be forced to face this neglect in short order.

In the last five years, three men died whose lives as citizens and as scientists provide a model for the citizens and scientists who are concerned with the four critical issues confronting society today: racism, sexism, militarism, and Social Darwinism. These men were T.C. Schneirla and his students, Daniel S. Lehrman and Herbert G. Birch. All three were aware of themselves as members of society. They rejected the notion that they were more independent of personal value systems and attitudes than other members of society. At the same time, they saw the scientific method as the best way of approaching the problems of people: they did so with humanism and commitment. They defined their scientific work in the most rigorous fashion and above all were conscious of how society formed and informed them, and how they might form and inform society. The four people who have contributed to this volume have tried to do likewise in the same spirit of commitment and humanism within the rigors of the scientific method.

BIBLIOGRAPHY

Aronson, L. R., E. Tobach, J. S. Rosenblatt and D. S. Lehrman, (eds.). *Selected Writings of T. C. Schneirla.* San Francisco: W. H. Freeman, 1972.

Birch, H. G. and J. D. Gussow. *Disadvantaged Children.* Health Nutrition and School Failure. New York: Harcourt Brace and World, Inc., 1970.

Lehrman, D. S. Semantic and conceptual issues in the nature-nurture problem. In *Development and Evolution of Behavior. Essays in Memory of T. C. Schneirla.* L. R. Aronson, E. Tobach, J. S. Rosenblatt and D. S. Lehrman, (eds.), San Francisco: W. H. Freeman, 1970, pp. 17-52.

Lehrman, D. S. Behavioral science, engineering and poetry. In *The Biopsychology of Development.* E. Tobach, L. R. Aronson and E. Shaw (eds.). New York: Academic Press, 1971, pp. 297-302.

Tobach, E. and L. R. Aronson. Theodore C. Schneirla: A Biographical note. In *Development and Evolution of Behavior. Essays in Memory of T. C. Schneirla.* L. R. Aronson, E. Tobach, J. S. Rosenblatt and D. S. Lehrman, (eds.). San Francisco: W. H. Freeman, 1970, pp. xi-xviii.

THE FOUR HORSEMEN

Genes, Intelligence, and Race

Howard Topoff

Support for this paper was provided by a grant (#1723) from the Research Foundation of the City University of New York. I thank Ethel Tobach, Irwin Herskowitz, and Lee Ehrman for reading the manuscript and offering valuable suggestions.

One of the most significant events formulating my thoughts about science resulted from a discussion that took place in my undergraduate freshman biology course. The class was debating whether the acellular organism *Euglena* is a plant or an animal. Some students argued that *Euglena* must be placed in the animal kingdom, because it has a flagellum and is motile. Others contended that it is a plant, because it contains chlorophyll and synethesizes high-energy phosphates by photosynthesis. The instructor of the class settled the issue by putting it to a vote. *Euglena* was elected to the animal kingdom by a clear majority, and the class was dismissed.

Several years passed before I fully appreciated the absurdity of our behavior in that class. After all, the aim of every scientific observation and experiment is not to impose our preferences on the physical and natural world, but to describe it with terminology and concepts that most accurately reflect it. However, because science is a human endeavor, we must always be extremely careful not to combine our own subjective beliefs with our scientific analyses. Otherwise, our conclusions about the world will always be based, at the very least, upon a distorted picture of natural phenomena. The magnitude of the problem becomes even greater, however, when a scientist mistakenly introduces personal bias in formulating conclusions about human behavior, because the consequences of this kind of distortion may be socially dangerous.

An excellent example of incorrect scientific interpretation, due in part to the incorporation of subjective considerations, is the current controversy as to whether there are inherited differences in intelligence among human races. A review of the now vast literature on this subject indicates that most of the controversy is centered around opposing theses that attempt to assess whether the contributions of genetic processes to intelligence are greater than the contributions of environmental influences, or vice versa. Although questions related to racial differences in intelligence have probably been discussed since human variation was first recognized, the amount of published material in both the scientific and popular media has recently increased substantially. And, as is well known, much of the most recent inundation of material is based upon theoretical conclusions stemming from the I.Q. bomb released by Jensen (1969), and from the fallout that continues to emanate from it (Eysenck, 1971).

Regardless of which side of the nature-nurture fence one sits on, the fact that the controversy exists means that at least three assumptions have been accepted. Briefly, these are: (1) that principles of population genetics have been properly used; (2) that intelligence can be defined in such a way that genetic analyses can be conducted; and (3) that the concept of race is a biologically valid taxonomic category. In this paper I will discuss these three assumptions.

POPULATION GENETICS AND THE STUDY OF DEVELOPMENT

Imagine for a moment that you were assisting Gregor Mendel as he conducted his pioneering crosses of inbred, homozygous garden pea plants. Mendel crossed plants having red flowers with those of the white variety; all of the offspring (the F_1 generation) had red flowers. Mendel's conclusion was that red flower color is inherited. Suppose you had asked Mendel how the hereditary factors (which we now call genes) produce flower color during the development of any one individual plant from the seed to the mature organism. Mendel's reply could only have been, "I don't know." The point is that in spite of Mendel's lack of knowledge of developmental genetics and the physiology of pigment formation, he was still able to state that flower color is inherited. The reason for this is that the term "inherited" as used by geneticists is a concept that results from the analysis of breeding experiments conducted with populations of organisms, and its typical application consists of the correlation between the distribution of observed characteristics (phenotypes) in a population and the distribution of the inferred underlying genotypes. As classically used, the term "inherited" does not apply to the development of characteristics in any particular individual of the population.

To illustrate this point, let's conduct a hypothetical breeding experiment (Fig. 1). I will begin with a distribution of individuals exhibiting a quantitatively varying trait (in this case, body weight). The mean weight of the population is 150 pounds (Fig. 1A). As parents of the next (i.e., the first filial) generation, I will designate a subpopulation of individuals who vary in body weight between 160 and 180 pounds, and with a mean weight of 170 pounds (Fig. 1B). Therefore, the difference in mean weight between the entire population and the parental subpopulation is

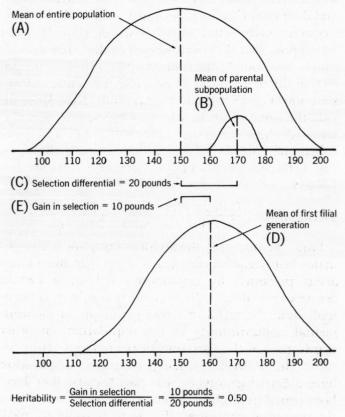

Heritability = $\dfrac{\text{Gain in selection}}{\text{Selection differential}} = \dfrac{10 \text{ pounds}}{20 \text{ pounds}} = 0.50$

Fig. 1. Weight-frequency distribution of hypothetical population, used to calculate estimates of heritability.

20 pounds. Thus, by selecting a subpopulation with a mean weight of 170 pounds to be the parents of the next generation, we are attempting to increase the mean weight from 150 pounds in the first generation to 170 pounds in the second generation. In the terminology of population genetics, this is called the selection differential (Fig. 1C). After the parents mate, and their offspring become adult, we plot the weight-frequency distribution of the offspring (Fig. 1D). Let us suppose that the mean weight of this filial generation is 160 pounds. This means that although our selection differential was 20 pounds, our actual gain in selection (Fig. 1E) was only 10 pounds. Now if we divide the actual gain in selection by the selection differential, the result is an approximation of a measure called "heritability." Thus, in the example shown in Fig. 1, the heritability of body weight is calculated as follows:

$$\text{Heritability} = \frac{\text{Gain in selection}}{\text{Selection differential}} = \frac{10\,\text{pounds}}{20\,\text{pounds}} = 0.50$$

From the time that the architects of population genetics first began to consider the fact that most characters possessed by populations exhibit a certain degree of variability, the variability has been conceptualized as the result of either genotypic or environmental nonuniformity in the population. In other words, part of the variation in phenotypes arises because the individuals comprising the population have different genotypes, and part because they have been reared in slightly different environments. Thus, the reasoning continues, if it were possible to make the environment of all individuals in the population the same, then all of the phenotypic variability must necessarily be due to the underlying genetic variation among the individuals. In our hypothetical example (Fig. 1), a heritability index of 0.50 is interpreted to mean that 50 percent of the variance in weight is due to genetic differences among the individuals of the population, and 50 percent is due to environmental differences.[1] In general, whenever attempts are made to assess the relative contributions of genetics and environment to phenotypic variation, the index that has been the conceptual tool of choice in making this assessment is heritability.

The heritability index can vary from a value of 0.0, in which case all phenotypic variation within a population is considered to be caused by environmental factors, to a maximum value of 1.0, in which case all variation is considered to be genetic in origin. The following examples will illustrate these two extreme cases.[2]

First, suppose we have a population of people who lack the sequence of DNA nucleotides necessary to specify the amino acids involved in the synethesis of insulin. Let us also assume that some of these indi-

[1] Most psychological studies actually use estimates of heritability. The complete mathematical formula for heritability in population genetics is considerably more complicated than the one presented in this discussion. It includes not only additive genotypic variance and environmental variance, but also variance due to assortative mating, dominance deviation, and epistasis (the interaction among genes at different chromosomal loci).

[2] Although indices of heritability are typically calculated on the basis of traits that vary quantitatively, I am using qualitative traits for the purpose of these examples.

viduals regularly take insulin and therefore do not exhibit the diabetic phenotype. If we select these phenotypically "normal" individuals to be the parents of the next generation, and then analyze the phenotypes of their offspring in an environment without insulin, we would find that all of the offspring exhibit the diabetic phenotype. Thus, in this case, the gain in selection from the parental generation to the first filial generation is 0.0, which is therefore also the value of the heritability index. This is interpreted to mean that the phenotypic variation (i.e., the presence of some individuals with diabetes and some without it) of the parental population was simply due to differences with respect to one aspect of their environment—namely the presence or absence of insulin.

To illustrate a heritability index with a value of 1.0, we will consider the ABO system of blood classification. In this case, we start with a population of individuals in which the A, B, AB, and O blood types are equally represented. We then select only those individuals that have the recessive O blood type to be the parents of the next generation. When the subsequent analysis is conducted, all of the individuals in the first filial generation will be found to have the O type of blood. In this case, therefore, the gain in selection is equal to the selection differential, the heritability index has a value of 1.0, and the variation in blood types is considered to be determined exclusively by the diverse genotypes of the individuals.

In all of the above cases, note that the indices of heritability were always calculated from the results of breeding experiments conducted with populations of organisms. This means that the heritability index cannot be used to answer the important question that you posed to Mendel, namely how does any given phenotype develop from the interaction between genes and environment in any one individual of the population. This is an important point to keep in mind when interpreting the vast literature on the inheritance of intelligence (or of any characteristic at any level of biological or psychological organization), because there is a tendency among laymen and scientists alike to think that the higher the heritability index (in a population, of course) the more difficult it is to alter by environmental manipulation the development of a particular trait in any individual of the population. Eysenck (1971), in his book entitled *Race, Intelligence and Education,* makes this error when he assumes that a heritability index of 0.8 for I.Q. scores means that 80 percent of an individual's intelligence is determined by genes. He then uses this incorrect application of heritability to argue against special educational programs for people with below-average I.Q.

In view of Eysenck's conclusion, and those of other scientists who consistently misuse principles of population genetics, there is a real need to constantly re-iterate the fact that heritability is a property of populations and not of traits (Hirsch, 1963, 1970). To illustrate this, let us return to our original breeding experiment (Fig. 1). Suppose we had reared the offspring of the parental generation with inadequate food. Then their mean adult body weight might have been only 150 pounds. In this case the gain in selection would be 0.0, which would also be the value of the heritability index. This shows that the heritability index, which to many people is supposed to indicate the degree to which environmental factors are not involved, changes when the individuals are in fact reared under different environmental conditions. Now if we have a measure that is supposed to indicate the lack of environmental contribution to a particular phenotype, and if this same measure changes when a population of individuals is reared under different environmental conditions, then obviously the measure is meaningless as a tool for assessing the relative contributions of genetic and environmental factors to phenotypic development.

Another frequent misconception about heritability is that if the heritability index is high for phenotypic variance *within* any population, then it must also be high for the variation that exists *between* populations. Thus, Eysenck maintains that if the variance in I.Q. among members of a given population exhibits a high index of heritability, then the chances are good that racial differences in I.Q. are also strongly genetically determined. The fact is, however, that regardless of the magnitude of the heritability index for phenotypic variance within any population, no extrapolation is automatically possible concerning the relative contribution of genes and environment to phenotypic variation between populations. The best illustration of this point that I have found is the football field analogy presented by Colman (1972). Consider two sets of fields. The length of each field in the first set is 100 feet, but the width of each varies by a few feet. In the second set the length of each field is 500 feet, and again the widths vary by a few feet. Within each of the two populations of fields, the variance in area is determined entirely by differences in width. However, the difference between the mean areas of the two populations is obviously determined primarily by their differences in length. As Colman points out in this analogy, even if the variance in I.Q. scores within each of two populations were due entirely to genetic factors, the average difference between the two populations could still be due entirely to environmental factors.

Once we understand that the correct contextual use of heritability indices is in analyzing the results of breeding experiments conducted with populations, and not in explaining the development of traits in individuals, we are then in a position to understand the influence that the concept of heritability has had on our thinking about the relationship between genes and environment, both in population studies and during individual development. First, we have seen that the heritability index can vary from a value of 0.0, when all phenotypic variation is considered to be caused by environmental differences, to a maximum value of 1.0, in which case all phenotypic variation is said to be caused by genotypic differences. Yet, all population geneticists agree that regardless of the magnitude of the heritability index, all traits within an individual develop from an interaction between genes and environment. Furthermore, recent advances in experimental embryology have shown that the gene-environmental interactions characteristic of developmental processes are so inextricably interdependent that it is impossible to quantify and distinguish the relative contributions of genetic and environmental factors (Bell, 1971; Harris, 1970; Market and Ursprung, 1971; Schultz, 1965). I maintain that if the experimental embryologists are correct, then it is also impossible to parcel out the roles of genetics and environment in studies of phenotypic variability within or between populations. I will begin, therefore, with a brief discussion of what I believe to be the emerging conceptualization of development, in the hope that this will provide a basis for reinterpreting the concept of heritability.

The idea that individual development arises from an interaction between genes and environment is certainly no new. However, if one critically analyzes the notion of this interaction as held by many behavioral scientists, it is clear that development is still pictured as the classical unfolding of a genetic potential (or blueprint) as programmed in the DNA, with the role of the environment determining to what extent the potential will be realized (see, for example, Cooper, 1972; Eibl-Eibesfeldt, 1970; Manning, 1972). As far as I can tell, the problem with this formulation of development does not lie with the conceptualization of a gene, which can always be defined in terms of the actual sequence of nucleotides. Instead, the difficulty stems from the interpretation of the term "environment," and from the idea as to what constitutes an interaction. The environment has traditionally been thought of as factors that clearly originate outside of the organism, such as temperature, humidity, and light, although many internal factors, such as hormones, have also been recognized. But in both cases, the *contributions* of these "classical" environmental factors to growth, differentiation, organogenesis, and other developmental processes are often still conceived as being distinct and separable from the *contributions* of the genes. Although many experimental embryologists and several comparative psychologists (Schneirla, 1956, 1957; Tobach, 1972) have argued that the notion of genes and environment interacting in a purely additive manner is not consistent with the known facts of developmental processes, many behavior geneticists still cling to this naive abstraction.

At the time of fertilization, most organisms consist of a diploid set of chromosomes surrounded by nucleoplasmic and cytoplasmic environment, and if anything must be considered to be passed from parents to offspring, it is this interacting system. Fertilized eggs are not homogeneous cells. The cytoplasmic environment surrounding the chromosomes is a very complex and heterogeneous mixture of biochemicals, organelles, and other substances, all distributed in a nonrandom and nonuniform way throughout the egg (Market and Ursprung, 1971). The nature of this initial biochemical environment is also somewhat unique, because many of the cytoplasmic substances, including the cellular machinery for polypeptide synthesis and energy-producing metabolism, are present in the egg prior to fertilization. This means that the very first stages of developmental cleavage are produced to a large extent by the interactions between genes and a biochemical environment that is very different from that which will be present at a later stage of development, when RNA produced by the genome of the new individual is translated into biochemical products.

The activation of genes during development can be brought about by several different processes. In many species, a group of chemicals called histones are linked to the sugar-phosphate backbone of the double-stranded DNA molecule, and in this state are capable of repressing DNA-dependent RNA synthesis (Huang and Kleiman, 1971). Chemical substances from the nucleoplasm or cytoplasm can interfere with the chemical linkage between histones and DNA, and the result is usually an abrupt increase in RNA transcription (Busch, 1965). The point to be emphasized here is that substances distinct from the genes are necessary for RNA transcription to occur, and these substances can be conceptualized as components of the genes' environment. Furthermore, as soon as the newly transcribed RNA enters the cytoplasm and becomes translated into polypeptide and protein molecules, the cytoplasmic environment surrounding the genes changes. This new biochemical environment then brings about the selective activation (or repression) of different segments of the DNA. Thus, from the earliest stages of development onwards, a sequence of reciprocal and interdependent interactions exists, with genes and cytoplasm constantly providing both positive and negative feedback to each other. Because the activity of every gene ultimately produces biochemical products that alter the environment of that same gene, it is wrong to conceptualize these early developmental processes merely as the unfolding of an inherited blueprint, under the "supervision" of a given and static environment.

At all stages of development, nucleocytoplasmic interactions are influenced by many factors that originate outside the organism. Depending upon the species and the level of organization of the characteristic under study, the particular factors (such as temperature, humidity, light, sound, etc. will differ in importance at different times during development. But even these "classical" environmental factors should not be considered as static inputs to the developing system. Light, for instance, does not just passively illuminate an embryo. It is a source of energy which, if it is to influence development at all, must be absorbed into the existing system (Schneirla, 1957; Tobach, 1972) and become integrated into the many levels of other gene-evironmental interactions that are in progress. Somewhat later during development, biochemicals such as tissue products and hormones also become important factors. When neural tissue appears in the embryo, its development can also be influenced by numerous kinds of neural experiential affects, including simple conditioning and more complex processes of learning. Finally, we must also consider the social environment that is present at every stage of development. Included in this broad category are the nutritional state of the mother, the sociology of the family, the education of the child, and many additional cultural factors.

It is obviously impossible in this brief discussion to specify a complete list of factors contributing to development, and their relative effectiveness in different species, and at different stages of embryogeny. The problem is compounded by the fact that those factors which are important during the earliest stages of development (e.g., cytoplasmic biochemicals) remain important throughout subsequent stages (Tobach, 1972). Furthermore, the contribution of almost every factor is influenced to some degree by every other factor. Thus, the biochemical, physiological, and neuro-anatomical condition of the organism at any stage of development determines the kinds of neural modifiability that can occur, but the consequences of such neural transmission are that the biochemical and physiological state of the organism is automatically altered. Factors such as temperature and light can affect the metabolic machinery of the organism at any stage of development. Hormones alter biochemical processes, in part by their ability to initiate gene activation (Schimke, 1967). In short, an alteration of any factor at any stage of development can have a pronounced effect on all existing systems. Because developmental processes are based upon a necessary interdependence of sequential events, the effectiveness of any input will depend not only upon the biochemical, physiological, and anatomical state of the organism at that moment, but also upon everything that has happened to the developing individual during all preceding stages.

The above formulation of development, although necessarily brief, nevertheless, can aid considerably in reversing the traditional tendency of laymen and scientists alike to classify individual characteristics as a product of "so much genetics and so much environment." To illustrate this point, I will use a hypothetical, but reasonable, example. Suppose we find that an enzyme is typically synthesized at a particular time during development. Prior to that time, the segment of DNA specifying the amino acids of the enzyme does not transcribe RNA. Biochemical analysis shows that RNA transcription depends upon a specific cytoplasmic substance that must cross the nuclear membrane and interfere with the chemical linkage between a certain class of histones and the DNA segment. The cytoplasmic substance only crosses the nuclear membrane when a particular hormone is secreted into the cytoplasm and is present above a certain concentration. Finally, the secretion of the hormone is mediated by the intensity of light falling on the embryo.

Here we have a relatively simple series of interdependent sequential events leading to the synthesis of an enzyme. My question is: what percentage of this biochemical trait is a result of genetic processes, and what percentage is due to the environment? It should be obvious that the question is meaningless! Furthermore, the example suggests that behaviorists may do well to reconsider not only the feasibility of quantifying genetic and environmental factors, but also the utility of distinguishing between them in the first place. No factor, regardless of where it originates, can influence development until some part of its contained energy becomes integrated into the interacting system. As a result, what purpose is served by arguing whether the influence of any factor during development is an external or internal one? No gene can be activated (or repressed) without the action of some factor external to the gene. So what is gained by arguing whether any developmental process is genetic or environmental? If the goal of behavior geneticists is to clarify how characteristics representing all levels of biological and psychological organization develop, then the role of every possible factor and the interactions among them should be investigated. It is perfectly reasonable to inquire how histones, DNA, RNA, ribosomes, enzymes, hormones, temperature, sound, learning, nutrition, family life, and even language influence development, and how alterations of these (and any other) factors result in corresponding changes in developmental processes. But these studies can and should proceed without having to specify which factors are genetic and which are environmental. To do otherwise not only retards the attainment of our goal, but it indicates our lack of understanding about development.

In the past, when a particular trait was said to be genetically determined, this usually implied that environmental factors were not involved in influencing its developmental outcome. But as we have just seen, such statements fail to appreciate the degree of interdependence between genes and the many kinds of possible environmental factors. If we accept the conceptualization of development discussed above, then all characteristics, whether biochemical, physiological, anatomical, or behavioral, must develop from a dynamic and inseparable interaction of genes and environment.

This conceptualization of development throws the concept of heritability into its proper perspective. Recall Mendel's experiment with the garden pea. He planted a population of seeds and reared the seedlings under the same conditions of light and water. In spite of this "equal" treatment, however, the adult plants exhibited pronounced variability: some had red flowers and some had white flowers. Mendel concluded, therefore, that flower color is genetically determined (i.e., it is heritable). His conclusion was based upon the rationale for studying heritability, namely that if the environment of all individuals of a population is the same, then any resulting pheno-

typic variability must be due to the genotypic variation among the individuals. But, if, as we have seen,
the environment can be conceptualized to include not
only "classical" factors such as light and water, but
also ions, enzymes, hormones, and many other factors that originate both inside and outside the organism, then it is clear that no two individuals can possibly be reared in the same environment. Because
every individual plant begins development as a
unique genome surrounded by a unique biochemical
environment, it is inevitable that the development of
every individual will proceed along a different
course. In the case of the pea plants, the interactions
between the genes and environment in individuals of
the two varieties produced contrasting adult phenotypes with respect to flower color, even though all individuals of both varieties were given the same
amount of light and water. As a result, the only valid
conclusion from Mendel's experiment is that light
and water were not responsible for the variability in
flower color. Studies of heritability, therefore, can
only point out that certain factors are not responsible
for the observed phenotypic variability. Only studies
of how the many levels of gene-environmental interaction differ among all individuals of a population
can elucidate the basis for phenotypic variability.

POPULATION GENETICS AND THE STUDY
OF INTELLIGENCE

Psychologists generally agree that intelligence is
such a multifaceted characteristic that no single defi-

nition of it is possible. Even Alfred Binet, the founder of the first widely used scale of intelligence, gave up trying to base his studies on a concrete definition of intelligence, and concentrated instead on devising tasks that could be performed by a majority of normal children of a given age (Vandenberg, 1968). No one knows exactly how many specific abilities are subsumed under the heading of intelligence, but the number proposed ranges up to 120 (Guilford, 1959). Tests of intelligence are designed to sample the performances of individuals with respect to their versatility in the use of many symbolic processes. They are constructed so that most scores fall close to a mean value of 100, which represents a level of achievement typical for the individual's age group.

Intelligence tests have been administered en masse in this country for many years, and numerous comparisons have been made among the performances of many ethnic populations. It is now generally known that the Black population of the United States has a mean I.Q. score that is 15 points below the mean of the White population. Many biologists and psychologists have repeatedly maintained that too much emphasis is placed on comparing populations only with respect to their mean scores on these tests, because such analyses provide no opportunity for understanding the bases for the differences in scores among individuals within each population (Hirsch, 1970; Pettigrew, 1964). Thus, although many studies of intelligence have pointed out the contrasting mean I.Q. scores between Blacks and Whites, few analyses have focused our attention on the fact that the range of performance within both populations is approximately equal. In fact, the distribution of scores on these tests is such that 15 percent of the Black population actually surpasses the performance of 50 percent of the White population (Goldsby, 1971).

In spite of the overwhelming evidence that individual differences in I.Q. scores within any one human population exceed the differences between these same populations, the main thrust of most studies of intelligence is still based upon the use of estimates of heritability for assessing the relative contribution of genes and environment in producing the *average* differences between populations. In all of these studies, the justification is based on the assumption that the environment for individuals from both populations has been equalized. But because heritability is basically a negative concept, in that it can only suggest which factors are not important for the development of phenotypic variability, we should seriously question the significance of this measure in studies of intelligence. This point is illustrated by the fact that estimates of the heritability of intelligence are typically derived from studies of identical (i.e., monozygotic) and fraternal (dizygotic) twins reared together and apart. In these studies, the high correlation of intelligence scores between identical twins is interpreted as resulting entirely from their genetic similarity. But identical twins also share an entire array of environmental factors, including those operative before birth and between birth and adoption (Colman, 1972).

In all studies involving the use of heritability indices, we must always inquire as to which specific environmental factors have been equalized. Thus, if differences are observed between the mean I.Q. scores of Black and White children from the same school, the only conclusion possible is that factors other than the exposure of the students to a common core of educational material are responsible for their contrasting performance on I.Q. tests. It is absurd to use this information for concluding that the differences in mean scores are due to differences in the genes of the individuals from the two populations. Classroom instruction is certainly an important environmental factor, but it is only an extremely minute part of the sum total of biochemical, biological, psychological, and sociological factors that could differ at all stages during the development of individuals from the two populations.

In my previous discussion of development, I pointed out the impossibility of quantifying the role of genetics and environment during development, and I used the synthesis of an enzyme as an example. It should be obvious that if the task is impossible for an enzyme, it is inconceivable to attempt such a categorization for intelligence, a behavioral characteristic which represents one of the most complex levels of biological and psychological organization.

In concluding this section, I would like to add that because intelligence is so complex, "normal" intelligence must involve the "normal" development of a huge number of organ systems and physiological processes. As a result, when viewed in its totality, looking for the genetic basis of intelligence is almost tantamount to looking for the genetic basis of life. As a result, we should not be misled by studies which purport to elucidate the role of genes in intelligence by calling attention to the fact that some mutations (such as the one resulting in the metabolic disorder known as phenylketonuria) result in lower intelligence. By way of analogy, consider a hypothetical mutation that results in the absence of an enzyme involved in a vital metabolic process, with the result that the individual dies. We could not interpret this by concluding that we have found the genetic basis for life.

The Concept of Race

Every species of plant and animal exhibits some degree of variation among the individuals comprising it, and the human species is no exception. Throughout recorded history, all known human societies have always had methods of distinguishing themselves as a group from other groups. The criteria used to make these distinctions, however, have changed in accordance with the nature of available information. Before principles of Darwinian evolution were widely understood, societies used such readily available measures as geography, religion, and outwardly visible morphological characteristics. But then came the advent of sophisticated scientific techniques derived, in part, from principles of population genetics. As a result, societies found it very easy to misuse these valid scientific concepts, and to adapt them to their preconceived societal framework.

The application of rigorous scientific methodology to elucidating the processes of human evolution began only during the middle of the 18th century. Prior to that period, one of the principal obstacles to a full appreciation of evolutionary processes was the lack of sufficient knowledge about the vast amount of time necessary for evolution to occur. After all, it was as late as 1650 that Archbishop James Usher put forth his now famous biblical chronology, in which the date of the creation of the world was set at approximately 4000 B.C. Today, of course, we know that the ancestry of even the human species dates from protohominid populations that diverged from other primate lines well over 15 million years ago (Le Gros Clark, 1959; Pfeiffer, 1969). The phenotypic dissimilarity that is so characteristic of present-day *Homo sapiens* has prompted scientists from many disciplines to attempt to devise objective methods of subdividing the human species. The category "race" has been the classificatory construct most often used for this purpose. Because the study of human variation is only a small part of a broader endeavor by taxonomists to order the staggering diversity of the entire animal kingdom, it is with systematic zoology that we begin our analysis of the concept of race.

The principal aim of systematics is to describe the diversity of living things, and to explicate the evolutionary processes responsible for such diversity. One of the first steps in achieving this goal is the classification of organisms: that is, the placing of organisms into groups on the basis of their similarity and evolutionary relationships. At the present time there are approximately 18 taxonomic categories utilized to classify organisms (Fig. 2), and these 18 categories can be separated into three conceptually different groups.

THE MAJOR TAXONOMIC CATEGORIES

Kingdom

Phylum

Subphylum

Superclass

Class

Subclass

Superorder

Order

Suborder

Superfamily

Family

Subfamily

Tribe

Genus

Subgenus

SPECIES

Subspecies

Fig. 2. Major taxonomic categories used by systematists in classifying organisms.

We will consider first the taxonomic category of species. A species is a group of populations of organisms that interbreed successfully among themselves and which are reproductively isolated from other such groups of populations (May, 1963). Reproductive isolation is a condition by which interbreeding among species is prevented, thus maintaining the distinctiveness of the species' gene pools. The phenomena that prevent interbreeding between species are termed reproductive isolating mechanisms, some of which are outlined in Table 1.

Of particular importance for this discussion is the fact that the principal criterion for designating species is establishing that the populations under study are reproductively isolated, and regardless of which groups of invertebrate or vertebrate animals are being investigated, the criterion remains the same. But whenever any of the taxonomic categories above and

TABLE 1
Classification of Isolating Mechanisms
(based upon Mayr, 1963)

1. Mechanisms that prevent interspecific crosses
   (a) Potential mates do not meet (seasonal and habitat isolation)
   (b) Potential mates meet but do not mate (behavioral isolation)
   (c) Copulation attempted but it is unsuccessful (mechanical isolation)
2. Mechanisms that reduce the success of interspecific crosses
   (a) Sperm transfer occurs but egg is not fertilized (mortality of gametes)
   (b) Egg is fertilized but zygote dies (zygote mortality)
   (c) Zygote produces hybrid of reduced viability (hybrid inviability)
   (d) Hybrid is viable but sterile (hybrid sterility)

below the species level is considered, the situation is entirely different. All taxonomic categories above the species (Fig. 2) consist of groups of related species that are separated from other such groups by some degree of phenotypic discontinuity. Thus, while the species category is based primarily on the distinctiveness of populations, higher taxonomic groupings are collective concepts, emphasizing similarity and evolutionary relationship. For example, a genus is a taxonomic category composed of a group of species that are descendent from a common ancestor (i.e., they are monophyletic), and which are phenotypically distinct from other such species groups. But a taxonomist classifying species of flatworms into genera would have to utilize different characteristics and criteria than would a taxonomist classifying organisms representing a different stage of evolutionary history, such as primates. Therefore, because there are no universal characters that define generic rank (Mayr, 1969), each investigator must decide whether the gap between groups of species is sufficient to warrant generic separation. Likewise, nonarbitrary definitions of all higher taxonomic categories also cannot be stipulated. Thus, the basic operations of the taxonomist almost always include an element of arbitrariness, with the result that it is usually possible to interpret biochemical, physiological, morphological, and behavioral information in ways that enable alternative classifications to be devised.

For the present discussion, the taxonomic category that is most important conceptually is the subspecies, because this is the category that the concept of race on the human level most closely approximates. The subspecies, which is the only category below the level of the species that is recognized in the International Code of Nomenclature, is regularly used in dealing with the fact that most species of animals consist of numerous local populations, some of which are visibly different from each other. Such species are said to be polytypic, and the local populations are designated as subspecies (Mayr, 1963, 1969). Now, in order for populations to be considered subspecies, their phenotypic distinctiveness must be sharply demarcated. This is a very important point, because there is another type of population variation that is formed when a species is composed of a series of geographically contiguous populations in which a given characteristic changes gradually throughout the range of the species. The term "cline" is used for this type of variation, but it is not a taxonomic category. The predominant reason for the existence of clines is that environmental selective factors vary along geographical gradients, and the population's phenotypic characters change accordingly. In addition, gene flow among adjacent populations serves to smooth out any incipient genetic distinctiveness.

Clinal variations occur in practically all continental species that have ranges extending through more than one climatic zone, and they may include gradual changes in characteristics at any level of structural or functional organization. In all cases, however, it is the character that varies clinally, and not the population. Any given population may be part of as many clines as it has visible characters, and it is the very fact that clinal gradients of different characters within a single population often vary independently of each other that makes the cline unsuitable as a taxonomic category (Mayr 1969).

On the human level, many variations in characters once used to establish distinct classificatory schemes have, upon subsequent analyses, been shown to be clinal rather than discontinuous (Livingstone, 1962). The results of some of the most classical studies in physical anthropology, including analyses of body weight and height, have shown how common it is for anthropometric characters to vary clinally, and how meaningless it is to classify any segment of the population that is selected arbitrarily from the continuum (Biasutti, 1953; Newman, 1953; Schreider, 1950).

The above discussion, concerning the basis and terminology of infraspecific variation, is important for understanding the meaning and utility of the concept of race as it is usually applied in classifying populations of people. Human races are thought of as groups of people that can be grouped together on the basis of the fact that they possess an aggregate of common characteristics. The underlying assumption is that early in the evolution of human beings, each population settled in a particular habitat, and that under the exposure to different selective pressures they evolved numerous biochemical, morphological, physiological, and behavioral attributes that made each population uniquely adapted to its particular habitat. In other words, each population evolved a relatively distinct gene pool, so that entire blocks of traits evolved and changed concordantly within each population. According to this assumed scheme, the process of raciation is very similar to that of speciation; indeed, raciation has often been viewed as representing the initial stages of speciation, the ultimate result of which is the acquisition by the populations of complete genetic isolation. This concept of human races is similar to one of the ways in which some taxonomists have incorrectly used the category of subspecies; that is, a subspecies is sometimes considered to be synonymous with the term "incipient species." But the analogy between this usage of the subspecies concept and human populations is incorrect. Incipient species are populations in the process of acquiring increased reproductive isolation. The trend among human populations, however, is clearly towards decreasing reproductive isolation. Throughout the history of human beings, the importance of geographical barriers has steadily been reduced by nomadism and by increasing technological advances. Cultural barriers too, including those based upon language, religion, and social class, have become increasingly ineffectual. Thus, viewing the modifications of the numerous varieties of human populations from a historical perspective encompassing many thousands of years, all trends point to an ever-increasing gene flow among all populations (Hiernaux, 1964; Osborn, 1971).

I now come to the last and only correct use of the taxonomic category subspecies, and the conceptualization of it that corresponds closely to the way in which the concept of race is most often used to subdivide the human species. As I cited earlier in this discussion, a subspecies is a population of a species inhabiting a geographical subdivision of the species' range, and differing taxonomically from all other such populations. Now, at this point we should recall that the problems encountered in classifying groups of species into higher taxonomic categories above the level of the species are also experienced in attempting to designate subspecies. The subspecies, like categories above the species level, is not a unit of evolution (Mayr, 1969), and the criteria used to designate alternative subspecific populations are arbitrary and inconstant. One problem confronting the taxonomist is choosing which characteristics to use for the comparison. Another problem is deciding the number of characteristics that must differ between two populations in order for them to be designated as distinct subspecies. Although all taxonomists agree that subspecies should not be designated on the basis of single characters, when multiple traits are used they often do not vary concordantly. This is very similar to the situation mentioned above for clines, in which traits that change gradually are also found to vary discordantly. Thus, depending upon how many characteristics and which particular ones are used, taxonomists can often create many different constellations of subspecies from any one species. As a result, many noted evolutionary biologists (e.g., Wilson and Brown, 1953) have urged that the concept of subspecies be dropped as a taxonomic category.

All of the difficulties encountered by zoological taxonomists in their attempts to designate subspecies of animals are compounded many fold when efforts are made to subdivide the human species. To see why this is so, let's start with the assumption that all existing human populations arose from only one ancestral hominid line that diverged from other primate stocks approximately 15 million years ago. At the present

time there are several notions concerning the course of
the evolution of the human species. Some anthropologists believe that human races are relatively recent out-
growths of the human phyletic tree, having originated
from ancestors that evolved in a linear fashion until the
divergence took place. Others contend that races are
more ancient, and that each race had its own ancestral
progenitors who settled in a particular habitat and
evolved numerous biochemical, physiological, morphological, and behavioral attributes that made them
uniquely adapted to that habitat. The assumption
stemming from this idea is that each population
evolved a relatively unique gene pool, so that entire
blocks of traits evolved and changed concordantly. Recently, however, many physical anthropologists have
maintained that a rigorous analysis of the hominid fossil record provides still another interpretation of the
pattern of human evolution. It is becoming increasingly clear that fossil skeletal remains of humans
show as much variability as is discernible today (Kennedy, 1972; Barnicot, 1964). Specifically, when studies
are made of a series of specimens from within a particular prehistoric population, a degree of variation
is discovered that is comparable to that present
within a random sample of living populations. And
when comparisons are made between ancestral populations that were separated geographically (during
the same time period), practically the same degree
of variation is found as between different populations living today. The resulting picture of human
evolution emerging from these findings is not one of
genetically isolated groups of individuals that dif-
ferentiated in localized geographical areas. It seems

that we can no longer cling to the notion that human beings ever consisted of genetically uniform populations with aggregate phenotypes. Instead, some degree of interbreeding must have occurred continually throughout human history, with the result that very few assemblages of genotypes have remained in isolation long enough to produce an appreciable measure of homogeneity. The reason for this is that in the past, and even more in recent times, any trends toward adaptive specialization were offset by repeated migrations of entire populations, and by man's increasing capability to alter the environment in accord with his requirements (Hiernaux, 1964, Kennedy, 1972). Such anthropological analyses illustrate that the evolution of human beings cannot be visualized within the framework of the classical evolutionary tree-like pattern, in which a single basal trunk gave rise to distinct branches. Instead, the biological history of *Homo sapiens* is probably best conceptualized as an immense network or reticulum, in which populations that tended to diverge from the ancestral mass were inevitably reincorporated into it soon afterwards. The extent to which such population mixture occurred in the past history of the human species and continues to occur indicates that a systematic subdivision of the human species is impossible.

Part of the reason for this interpretation having taken so long to be appreciated is that only a relatively few phenotypic characteristics had been used by anthropologists in devising their classificatory schemes, and most of those traits were selected from the standpoint of convenience of measurement rather than from a knowledge of their importance in contributing to evolutionary adaptation. The fact is that the more characters used to classify the human species into distinct subspecific populations, the more difficult the task becomes. And if this trend continues, it is clear that any future attempts at a formal and rigid classificatory scheme are doomed to failure before they begin.

I must emphasize at this point that my argument against the taxonomic construct race does not drag along with it a denial of genotypic and phenotypic variation within the human species. On the contrary, interbreeding among human beings is certainly not 100 per cent species-wide, and populations do exist that contain gene frequencies differing from that of other populations. This diversity is real, and it will remain so regardless of what happens to the concept of race. The suggestion by anthropologists, geneticists, and behaviorists to abolish the concept of race is not promulgated because it represents a liberal attitude and is therefore politically expedient. On the contrary, the point is simply that the concept of race does not accurately describe the variation that exists both within and among human populations. The word race implies a population of individuals in which large blocks of traits are exhibited together, and which are absent or different in other populations. But how many traits must be present together in one population in order to designate it as a race? The fact is that there are no objective rules for making these decisions. Linnaeus, the founder of formal classificatory science, proposed a taxonomic breakdown of the human species into four races: Europeans, Africans, Asians, and Americans. Today, one can find in the anthropological literature proposals by different scientists in which from 2 to 200 races are recognized (Osborne, 1971). The magnitude of the difficulty can be illustrated simply enough by considering human variation with respect to only a few biochemical traits associated with blood groupings. If we attempted to designate human races on the basis of the distributions of the genetic alleles that comprise the ABO blood groupings, we could recognize four distinct races: those with blood type A, B, O, and AB. But if we choose to use instead the genetic alleles that determine the distribution of the Rh group, we can only designate two different races, an Rh positive one and an Rh negative one. Furthermore, it is obvious that many individuals who are separated into different races on the basis of the ABO system would have to be classified in the same race with respect to the Rh system. Now what would the result be if we took into account the thousands of biochemical and morphological traits that every person possesses? Given the reticulum-like pattern of human evolution, we would not be surprised to find these traits varying quite discordantly among human populations, with the result that it would probably be possible to set up an almost limitless number of racial constellations. To complicate matters even more, what would happen if we decided to incorporate, together with the biochemical and morphological characteristics, behavioral attributes in our system of classification? It is often assumed that if differences at the biochemical level of organization can be demonstrated between two populations, there must also be corresponding differences between the populations with respect to every other level of organization, including behavior. The fallacy of this assumption stems from a failure to appreciate that characteristics at different levels of organization often evolve and change at quite different rates (Mayr, 1969). For instance, the serum proteins, hemoglobin, and karyotypes of humans are still quite similar to those of the great apes (Buettner-Janusch, 1966; Goodman, 1963; Zuckerkandl, 1963). The tremendous deviation between the apes and human beings was achieved by the evolutionary change of some traits to a greater extent than others. The fact that the development of behavioral characteristics is always influenced to a greater extent by environmental factors than biochemical or morphological traits, leads to the prediction that whatever degree of discordance is found among populations compared by the use of anatomical traits alone, the magnitude of the discordance will be even greater when behavioral characteristics are included. Furthermore, the more complex the behavior pattern, especially in terms of the number of interacting factors that contribute to its development, the less likely it will correlate with characteristics at simpler levels of organization. And what kinds of behavioral processes could be more complex than those subsumed under the heading of intelligence?

It seems that almost every month we read about another study showing that mean I.Q. scores differ between White and Black populations in the United States. Although most people accept the fact that the White population in this country represents a genetically heterogeneous mixture of people from all over Europe, few people realize that the Black population is no less heterogeneous. Even the Africans who were brought to North America as slaves originated from geographical areas as far apart as West Africa, Angola, and Madagascar. It requires only a little thought, therefore, to realize that the Black population represents as great a biological range as that found among European populations (Pettigrew, 1964). To lump all Blacks into one population on the basis of one biochemical trait that they have in common—the presence of melanin pigment—is ludicrous, because it illustrates a gross misunderstanding about differences in evolutionary rates among different traits in geographically separated populations. It would make just about as much sense to lump the human species together with all other vertebrates on the basis that they all have the blood pigment hemoglobin.

Every time I read about studies purporting to correlate skin color with intelligence, I can't help but wonder who it was that decided that skin color is *the* important variable to be used in these studies. After all, melanin pigment is only one of the thousands of biochemical traits that could be correlated with intelligence. Where are all the studies showing that among human populations intelligence varies concordantly with Rh factor, with the concentration of the enzyme glucose-6-phosphate dehydrogenase, with the weight of the pancreas, or with eye color. The fact that only skin color is used to correlate with scores on I.Q. tests implies that melanin pigment (and only melanin pigment) is inextricably linked through pleiotropic biochemical processes with verbal comprehension, numerical ability, perceptual speed, space visualization, reasoning, word fluency, and memory. It seems to me, however, that there is a more parsimonious explanation. Our society simply does not discriminate against people on the basis of blood type, enzyme concentration, pancreas weight, or eye color.

Some geneticists maintain that the magnitude of human variation is so great that if the concept of race did not exist it would have to be invented. I maintain, however, that the concept of race does not accurately reflect the pattern of diversity in any species of animal, and therefore it should be eliminated as a *scientific* classificatory category. There are ample classificatory terms available to taxonomists without the construct of race. If one is dealing with geographical varieties of a species that fit the subspecies model, then the term subspecies should be used. If a local population is found that has a unique chromosomal arrangement, then the term "karyotypic population" should be used.

On the human level, traits that vary quantitatively, including skin color, height, and weight, cannot be used to erect distinct populations, because it is meaningless to separate out any segment of a phenotypic continuum. When qualitative traits such as blood type are used, it is possible to designate distinct groups. In these cases, however, the term "population" should be used, not the construct of race. The concept of the population is eminently more objective than that of race, because it forces us to stipulate exactly which characteristics we are referring to. It is certainly possible to objectively designate populations that differ in gene frequencies with respect to blood types, enzyme systems, or any other traits that are distributed qualitatively. But we are left unbiasedly free to appreciate that the number of such human populations that can be designated may change for each trait considered, and when more than one trait is used at a time (Dobzhansky, 1962; Hirsch, 1970; Montagu, 1964). The notion of race, by contrast, is used in the literature of biology and psychology to conceptualize too many *different* kinds of infra-specific variation. To many people it still implies a fixed number of populations. As a result, if any trait is actually found to cut across our preconceived racial categories, the only option open is to dismiss the trait as unimportant. Thus, it should be clear that the term "population" is not just an equivalent substitute for the politically "loaded" concept of race. The concept of the population is quite different, because it is the only one that correctly and objectively reflects the genotypic and phenotypic variation that exists within the human species.

REFERENCES

Barnicot, N. A. Taxonomy and variation in modern man. In A. Montagu (Ed.), *The concept of race.* London: Collier Books, 1964. Pp. 180-227.

Bell, E. Information transfer between nucleus and cytoplasm during differentiation. In D. D. Davies and M. Balls (Eds.), *Control mechanisms of growth and differentiation.* Exp. Biol. Symp. no. 25. New York: Academic Press, 1971. Pp. 127-143.

Biasutti, R. *LeRazze i popoli della terra.* Turin:

Unione Tipografico-Editrice Torinese, Vol. 1, 2nd ed., 1953.

Buettner-Janusch, J. *Origins of man*. New York: John Wiley & Sons, 1966.

Busch, H. *Histones and other nuclear proteins*. New York: Academic Press, 1965.

Colman, A. M. 'Scientific' racism and the evidence on race and intelligence. *Race*, 1972, *14*, 137-153.

Cooper, J. B. *Comparative psychology*. New York: Ronald Press, 1972.

Dobzhansky, T. *Mankind evolving*. New Haven: Yale Univ. Press, 1962.

Eibl-Eibesfeldt, I. *Ethology*. New York: Holt, Rinehart and Winston, 1970.

Eysenck, H. J. *Race, intelligence and education*. London: Temple Smith, 1971.

Goldsby, R. A. *Race and races*. New York: The Macmillan Co., 1971.

Goodman, M. Man's place in the phylogeny of the primates as reflected in serum proteins. In S. L. Washburn (Ed.), *Classification and human evolution*. Chicago: Aldine Publ. Co., 1963. Pp. 204-234.

Guilford, J. P. Three faces of intellect. *Amer. Psychol.*, 1959, *14*, 469-479.

Harris, H. *Nucleus and cytoplasm*. Oxford: Clarendon Press, 1970.

Hiernaux, J. The concept of race and the taxonomy of mankind. In A. Montagu (Ed.), *The concept of race*. London: Collier Books, 1964. Pp. 29-45.

Hirsch, J. Behavior genetics and individuality understood. *Science*, 1963, *142*, 1436-1442.

Hirsch, J. 1970. Behavior-genetic analysis and its biosocial consequences. *Seminars in Psychiat.*, 1970,

2, 89-105.

Huang, R. C., and Kleiman, L. Specificities in the structure and function of interphase chromosomes. In D. D. Davies and M. Balls (Eds.), *Control mechanisms of growth and differentiation.* Exp. Biol. Symp. no. 25. New York: Academic Press, 1971. Pp. 93-115.

Jensen, A. R. How much can we boost I.Q. and scholastic achievement? *Harvard Educat. Rev.,* 1969, *39,* 1-123.

Kennedy, K. A. The paleontology of human populations. *The Biol.,* 1972, *54,* 97-114.

Le Gross Clark, W. E. *The antecedents of man.* New York: Harper & Row, 1959.

Livingstone, F. B. On the non-existence of human races. *Curr. Anthropol.,* 1962, *3,* 279-281.

Manning, A. *An introduction to animal behavior.* Reading: Addison-Wesley, 1972.

Markert, C. L., and Ursprung, H. *Developmental genetics.* Englewood-Cliffs: Prentice-Hall, 1971.

Mayr, E. *Animal species and evolution.* Cambridge: Harvard Univ. Press, 1963.

Mayr, E. *Principles of systematic zoology.* New York: McGraw: Hill Book Co., 1969.

Montagu, A. The concept of race. In A. Montagu (Ed.), *The concept of race.* London: Collier Books, 1964. Pp. 12-28.

Newman, M. T. The application of ecological rules to the racial anthropology of the aboriginal new world. *Amer. Anthropol.,* 1953, *53,* 311-327.

Osborn, F. Races and the future of man. In R. H. Osborne (Ed.), *The biological and social meaning of race.* San Francisco: W. H. Freeman & Co., 1971. Pp.

149-157.

Osborne, R. H. The history and nature of race classification. In R. H. Osborne (Ed.), *The biological and social meaning of race*. San Francisco: W. H. Freeman & Co., 1971. Pp. 159-170.

Pettigrew, T. F. Race, mental illness, and intelligence: A social psychological view. *Eugen. Quart.*, 1964, *11*, 189-215.

Pfeiffer, J. E. *The emergence of man*. New York: Harper & Row, 1969.

Schimke, R. T. Protein turnover and the regulation of enzyme levels in rat liver. *Nat. Cancer Inst. Monogr.*, 1967, *27*, 301-314.

Schneirla, T. C. Interrelationships of the "innate" and the "acquired" in instinctive behavior. In P. P. Grassé (Ed.), *L'Instinct dans le comportement des animaux et de l'homme*. Paris: Masson, 1956. Pp. 387-452.

Schneirla, T. C. The concept of development in comparative psychology. In D. B. Harris (Ed.), *The concept of development*. Minneapolis: Univ. Minnesota Press, 1957. Pp. 78-108.

Schreider, E. Geographical distribution of the body weight/body surface ratio. *Nature*, 1950, *165*, 286.

Schultz, J. Genes, differentiation, and animal development. Brookhaven Symp. Biol. no. 18, 1965, 116-147.

Tobach, E. The meaning of the cryptanthroparion. In L. Ehrman, G. S. Osmenn, and E. Caspari (Eds.), *Genetics, environment, and behavior*. New York: Academic Press, 1972. Pp. 219-237.

Vandenberg, S. G. The nature and nurture of intelligence. In D. C. Glass (Ed.), *Genetics*. New York:

Rockefeller Univ. Press, 1968, 3-58.

Wilson, E. O., and Brown, W. L. Jr. The subspecies concept and its taxonomic application. *Syst. Zool.*, 1953, 2, 97-111.

Zuckerkandl, E. Perspectives in molecular anthropology. In S. L. Washburn (Ed.), *Classification and human evolution*. Chicago: Aldine Publ. Co., 1963. Pp. 243-272.

Biology and Pop-Biology: Sex and Sexism

C. G. Gross

I'd like to thank N. Weisstein, Ethel Tobach, Iseli Krauss, Nancy Frost, and Ashton Barfield for providing information and encouragement in the preparation of this paper.

It is hardly news that women are oppressed. As a class they are exploited, abused, discriminated against, and generally put down. They are paid much less than men,[1] are scarcely represented in the professions,[2] and are generally relegated to service and clerical jobs.[3] They are absent from positions of power and responsibility in government, industry, and universities.[4] They are denied equal protection under the law—not just in marital law but in criminal law, property law, and welfare law as well (Schulder, 1970). They are used to sell virtually everything and are the chief dumping ground for plastic America.[5] And from the beginning of their lives women (and men) are told that all this is right and proper, is the way it's always been (true), and is the way biology (or God) made it to be. After all, women are, *by nature*, weak, flighty, emotional, unaggressive, irresponsible, unambitious, dependent, and generally inferior. This is not prejudice or superstition or chauvinism: oh no, it is supposed to be SCIENCE. Or is it mythology? Arguments justifying the status of women are often drawn from the study of primate behavior and from physiology. Let us examine some of these.

69

Myth #1: Dominance and leadership are characteristic of male primates whereas child care is an exclusively female function.

Among baboons, adult males are much larger, stronger, and more aggressive than adult females. (De Vore, 1965; Southwick, 1963; Jay, 1968). The troop leaders are invariably male. Although high-ranking females exist, they do so only by virtue of their (transient) liason with a high-ranking male. Males have virtually nothing to do with child-rearing and don't seem to recognize their own offspring. Although this pattern of male dominance is characteristic of many primate groups it is not an invariable one. For example, among howlers, night monkeys, titis, marmosets, tamarins, and even gibbons (an ape) the situation is rather different. The sexes tend to behave alike and there is little sign of sexual dominance or leadership. In fact, in many of these species the male holds and carries the infant all the time except during feeding (Mitchell, 1969; De Vore, 1965; Jay, 1968; Southwick, 1963). Furthermore, it has been suggested that the degree of male dominance in primates varies with the harshness of the environment (Russell & Russell, 1971). Thus, sexual differentiation in dominance and aggression is minimal, absent, or even reversed among species that live high in the trees, have few enemies, and have a plentiful food supply, such as titis and gibbons. By contrast, male dominance, aggression, and initiative are maximal among species that spend much of their time on the ground in a hostile environment, such as the Hamadryas baboon.

What is the lesson here? Is it that male dominance is natural for humans? Or is it that when the basic problems of defense and economics are solved, child-rearing by the male becomes "natural"? Both conclusions are absurd. We are neither baboons nor titis nor even chimpanzees. We are humans and the social relations of animals, even if they were not species-specific, have no relevance for the problems of human ethics and society. Do we really want to take the Hamadryas baboon as our social and ethical model?

Myth #2: "Male bonding" is a biological characteristic of primates which makes males uniquely fit for political leadership.

Tiger (1969, 1970) defines male bonding as a "relationship between two or more males such that they react differently to members of their bonding unit as compared to individuals outside of it." He claims it to be a major determinant of human society ("its spinal column"). However, "male bonding" has only been reported for a few primate species and even then usually tends to be transitory and to consist of an older male and a younger one or possibly two male siblings. Temporary "alliances" are found among both males and females. Although monogamous bonding is relatively rare, it is more common than "male bonding." The only universal social bond among monkeys and apes is between mother and child (De Vore, 1965; Jay, 1968; Mitchell, 1969; Russell & Russell, 1971; Southwick, 1963). There is no evidence that "male bonding" is characteristic of human society.

Myth #3: Women are unfit for responsible positions because of cycles of mood and performance as-

sociated with the menstrual cycle.

A common argument against allowing women to hold responsible positions in our society is that they are supposed to have monthly fluctuations in emotional behavior and cognitive performance associated with their menstrual cycle (Tiger, 1969, 1970). Thus, a woman in a critical position might be called upon to make some important decisions at "the wrong time of the month." In spite of this common belief, there is no evidence for a relationship between intellectual performance and menstrual cycle. Although only a few adequate studies have been carried out, they all failed to show any correlation between the phase of menstrual cycle and performance on tests of intelligence, academic performance, or perceptual-motor skills (Wickham, 1958; Sommer, 1972a, 1972b). On the other hand, there is considerable evidence for changes in emotional behavior and mood associated with the menstrual cycle. Correlations have been reported between menstrual cycle and tension, depression, and the incidence of accidents and suicide (Bardwick, 1971; Dalton, 1964; Sommer, 1972a).

However, for several reasons, these fluctuations of mood with menstrual cycle are inadequate justifications for disqualifying women from public responsibility. In the first place, such correlations were found, on the average, for only about half the sample of women tested. Even among these women, the amount of variation was often trivial as compared with the effects of other events in their lives. Certainly, the fluctuations in mood and performance of men and women correlated with their circadian (daily) cycle are far greater than that associated with the menstrual cycle in most women (for an extensive discussion of circadian rhythms, see Luce, 1970). Perhaps we should prevent our leaders from making any major decisions when they have been awakened in the middle of the night or have just flown across several time zones. Similarly, illness, even of a minor kind, would seem to have a more deleterious effect on most people than the onset of menses.[6] Finally, monthly cycles have also been demonstrated in men (Santorio, 1657 [apparently the earliest report of monthly cycles in men]; Ramey, 1972; Manson, 1965; Holberg, Hamburger, & Hillman, 1965), although on the average they involve very much smaller variations than those associated with the menstrual cycle (although they are large enough, apparently, for Japanese bus lines to adjust the route and schedules of their drivers to coincide with their monthly cycle).

Myth #4: Feminine and masculine personality characteristics are the results of genetics and hormones and are therefore totally resistant to environmental influences.

This is a mixture of several myths and half-truths. Sex ("male" and "female") should be distinguished from gender ("masculine" and "feminine"). Sex is a biological concept and consists of genetic sex (XX or XY chromosomes), hormonal sex (primarily estrogenic or androgenic), gonadal sex (ovaries or testes), morphology of the reproductive organs, and morphology of the genitals. Gender is a psychological and cultural concept. It is defined by society. Gender or psychosexual differentiation is a product of the interaction of biological sex and cultural factors

Normally, of course, the different aspects of biological sex and gender are closely correlated—in fact, causally related to each other. Genetic constitution determines hormonal levels in the developing organism which in turn guide the development of the gonads. The gonads then become the source of hormones which regulate the development of the reproductive organs and the external genitalia. The external appearance of the infant determines how it is treated and what is expected of it.

In order to weigh the potency of biological and social factors in the determination of gender it is instructive to examine cases in which the normal correlations among the components of biological sex and between sex and gender are absent (for discussions of the biology of sexual differentiation, see Money, 1965; Diamond, 1968; Young, 1961). This occurs in several abnormal human conditions (Money, 1961, 1965, 1970; Armstrong & Marshall, 1964).

The rarest is *true hermaphroditism*. True hermaphrodites are defined as having both active testicular and ovarian tissue. They are mostly genetically female but their external genitalia range from normal female to normal male. Most true hermaphrodites are brought up as boys and usually their adult gender— their sexual behavior and personality—agrees with the arbitrary assignment of sex at birth and their subsequent upbringing.

In the *testicular feminization syndrome* the genetic sex is male, as are the internal organs. But during the differentiation of external morphology, something goes wrong and these patients develop completely female genitals and breasts. Thus, they are genetically and gonadally male, but externally female. Their hormone levels tend to be intermediate between male and female. Since they look like normal females they are usually brought up as such. As adults, at least some of then are reported to have personalities and behavior well within the normal feminine range.

The *adrenogenital syndrome* is characterized by female genetic sex and female gonads. However, there is an abnormally high level of androgen secretion from the adrenal glands which produces masculinization of the external appearance of the body. The degree of masculinization depends on the point in development at which the disorder occurs. Almost invariably in these cases, gender is determined by upbringing. Patients reared as boys develop into normal men and patients reared as girls develop into normal women (even in cases with a penis-sized clitoris, an exaggerated masculine physique, excessive hirsutism, and a deep voice). However, when there is some uncertainty as to gender assignment at birth and the patients are brought up "provisionally" as boys or girls, ambiguity as to gender role often characterizes the adult.

These three syndromes demonstrate the extraordinary power that child-rearing practices can have in the determination of adult gender identity and behavior.[7]

Whither?

I am not claiming that there are no behavioral differences between males and females in infancy. Such differences, whatever their cause, are very real

(Bardwick, 1971; Maccoby, 1966). Some of them may even be constitutional (whatever that means). However, what is more important is the subsequent jamming and squeezing of boys and girls into rigid masculine and feminine roles and personalities. All the institutions of society, dominated as they are by sexist myths, act to exaggerate real or imagined differences between the sexes and to suppress differences within sexes. Sissies and even tomboys are persecuted by their peers and, at the least, hassled by adults. The "tomboy," the girl with intellectual, mechanical, or athletic inclinations, really gets into a double bind in late adolescence. At this point the conflict between personality and our standards of femininity becomes cruel and often devastating (Maccoby, 1970). For a woman to utilize fully her artistic and intellectual powers and yet to remain a normal woman (by her own and by society's standards) is indeed to be a superwoman. Further breakdown of legal, educational, and employment barriers for women will probably result in a few more superwomen. Adequate child-care facilities will make it possible for still more women to have both children and professional careers.

As important as this is, I don't think it should be our final or only goal. Certainly, to encourage the aggressive, selfish, tough-driving behavior that our society approves as "masculine" in more individuals, male or female, would be a mixed blessing. Rather, we should begin restructuring our institutions and our attitudes so that "masculine" and "feminine" can flower in both boys and girls and men and women. To deny men the "feminine" qualities of sensitivity, empathy, nurturance, interest in people and, above all, child-rearing, is just the parallel of the sexist myths that have oppressed and continue to oppress women (Weisstein, 1970, 1971).

FOOTNOTES

1. Women employed full time in 1970 earned 60% of the median salaries of men. This is not simply due to occupational differences: among sales workers, women workers earned 40.4% of the salaries of men, clerical workers 66.2%, and professional workers 64.2%. (U.S. Dept. of Labor, Women's Bureau, Fact sheet on the earnings gap, 1971.)

2. In 1964 women were 22% of the staff in colleges and universities, 6% of the physicians, 8% of the scientists, 3% of the lawyers, 1% of the engineers. (U.S. Dept. of Labor, Women's Bureau, Fact sheet on women in professional positions, 1966.)

3. In 1960 only 18% of working women were classified as professional, managers, officials, or proprietors whereas 56% were classified as clerical, service, and "private household." More than one-fifth of employed women college graduates fell in the latter class. (U.S. Dept. of Commerce, Bureau of Census, 1961.)
1961.)

4. Women comprise 22% of college faculties but only 9% are full professors. This latter figure drops below 1% at most "elite" schools. (Association of American University Women, Survey exploring sex discrimination on college campuses, 1971.)

5. See any magazine or walk into any drug or grocery store.

6. Dr. S. Aronson, former chief of the endocrine clinic at University Hospital, told the *N.Y. Times* (July 31, 1970, p. 33) "he saw no more than two or three women patients a year who are upset by the menstrual period. 'And it certainly doesn't compare with Addison's disease and a broken back, or having ileitis, a stroke and heart trouble' he said, referring to the afflictions Presidents Eisenhower, Kennedy and Johnson suffered."

7. In this discussion of intersexuality, I depend heavily on the findings and interpretations of J. Money.

REFERENCES

Armstrong, C. M., & Marshall, A. J. (Eds.). *Intersexuality in vertebrates including man.* Academic Press, 1964.

Bardwick, J. M. *Psychology of women.* Harper & Row, 1971.

Dalton, K. *The premenstrual cycle.* Thomas, 1964.

De Vore, I. (Ed.). *Primate behavior: Field studies of monkeys and apes.* Holt, Rinehart and Winston, 1965.

Diamond, M. *Perspectives in reproduction and sexual behavior.* Indiana, 1968.

Holberg, F., Hamburger, C. & Hillman, D. Spectral resolution of low-frequency, small-amplitude rhythms in excreted 17-ketosteroids; probable androgen-induced circaseptan desynchronization. *Acta Endocr. Suppl.,* 1965, *103,* 5-54.

Jay, P. C. (Ed.). *Primates: Studies in adaptation and variability.* Holt, Rinehart and Winston, 1968.

Luce, G. G. *Biological rhythms in psychiatry and medicine*. National Institute of Mental Health, 1970.

Maccoby, E. E. (Ed.). *The development of sex differences*. Stanford, 1966.

Maccoby, E. E. Feminine intellect and the demands of science. *Impact Sci. Soc.*, 1970, *20*, 13-28.

Manson, J.C. Cyclic variations of the frequency of neutrophil leucocytes with "androgen-induced" nucleus appendages in an adult man. *Life Sci.*, 1965, *4*, 329-334.

Mitchell, G. D. Paternalistic behavior in primates. *Psych. Bull.*, 1969, *71*, 399-417.

Money, J. Sex Hormones and other variables in human eroticism. In W. C. Young (Ed.), *Sex and internal secretions*. Williams and Williams, 1961.

Money, J. Psychosexual differentiation. In J. Money (Ed.), *Sex research: New developments*. Holt, Rinehart and Winston, 1965.

Money J. Sexual Dimorphism and homosexual gender identity. *Psych. Bull.*, 1970, *74*, 425-440.

Ramey, E. Men's cycles. *M.S.*, Spring, 1972, 8-14.

Russell C., & Russell, W. M. S. Primate male behavior and its human analogues. *Impact Sci. Soc.*, 1971, *21*, 63-74.

Santorio, S. *De statica medicina*, A Vlacc., 1657.

Schulder, D. B. Does the la oppress women? In R. Morgan (Ed.), *Sisterhood is powerful*. Vintage, 1970.

Sommer, B. Menstrual cycle change and intellectual performance. *Psychosom. Med.*, 1972, *34*, 263-269. (a)

Sommer, B. Perceptual motor performance, mood and the menstrual cycle. Paper read at Western Psychological Association Meetings, Portland, Oregon, April 27, 1972. (b)

Southwick, E. H. (Ed.) *Primate social behavior.* Van Nostrand, 1963.

Tiger, L. *Men in groups.* Random House, 1969.

Tiger, L. The possible biological origins of sexual discrimination. *Impact Sci. Soc.,* 1970, *20,* 29-44.

Weisstein, N. "Kinder Kuche, Kirche" as scientific law; Psychology constructs the female. In R. Morgan (Ed.), *Sisterhood is powerful.* Vintage, 1970.

Weisstein, N. *Psychology constructs the female, or the fantasy life of the male psychologist.* New England Free Press, 1971.

Wickham, M. The effects of the menstrual cycle on test performance. *Br. J. Psychiat.,* 1958, *49,* 34-41.

Young, W. C. (Ed.). *Sex and internal secretions.* Williams & Williams, 1961.

Brain Triggers Toward War?

John Gianutsos

One of the current vogues in dealing with social problems such as aggression is to look for a solution in the brain. The assumption is that aggression is an innate primary drive and that the organism possesses inborn centers or, in current terminology, pre-wired circuits innervating aggressive behavior. A corollary of conceiving aggression as a primary drive which is physiologically expressed by means of innate neural mechanisms is that aggressive behavior can be controlled by means of these neural mechanisms. Kenneth Clark is undoubtedly referring to this corollary when he proposes that we should look for a biochemical way to control aggressive tendencies in our leaders. This general approach has recently been applied to the treatment of "aggressive" individuals. It was on the basis of centers of function that psycho-surgery (prefrontal lobotomy, leucotomy, etc.) some decades ago was justified. More recently surgical intervention has become refined with the advent of microelectrode techniques (Delgado, 1966; Heath, 1963, 1964; Mark & Ervin, 1970; Mark, Ervin, Sweet & Delgado, 1969). Two aspects of this assumption will be considered further: first, the utility of assuming aggressive tendencies to be unitary drive states and, second, whether or not it makes sense to look for corresponding brain loci.

As a concept, aggression has been used very broadly, indeed so broadly that it can be said that one man's bread is another man's aggression. In its current usage the term has a variety of meanings for different people, and in some formulations, is applicable to almost all behavioral events. Very recently the sublimation of aggression has even been prescribed as a cure for international military problems (Lorenz, 1966). The use of aggression in this all-inclusive manner resembles earlier attempts to explain everything in terms of several or even one underlying drive, such as sex.

About fifteen years ago in psychology the number of acquired drives had multiplied to the point where one was reminded of the use of increasing numbers of instincts as explanatory concepts at the turn of the century (McDougall, 1960). Instead of ascribing a new instinct to an as yet unexplained observation, an acquired drive was invoked. Hebb (1955) incorporated Lindsley's (1951) concept of a nonspecific "arousal" system, possibly the reticular activating system (Magoun, 1952), to account for phenomena which could not be easily accomodated by a multiple drive theory (Brown, 1953). However, the emphasis continues to rest on a single explanatory concept; so that the seat of power was said to reside first in "instinct," then in "drive," and finally in "arousal" mechanisms.

These reductionistic theories are similar to the type of solution for aggression arrived at by Lorenz (1966). Lorenz argues that since aggression is an instinct which must eventually be expressed, the solution is to ensure that its expression is constructive, or at least, harmless. This solution is based on an oversimplified theoretical foundation.

The same kind of objection must be raised vis-a-vis another major class of solutions for aggression, namely those which advocate chemical or electrical brain stimulation. All these proposals utimately depend on the assumption that there are localizable brain centers for aggression. In recent years the concept of centers in the brain has yielded to the formulation of "systems" of nerve trunks controlling complex functions, but the underlying theme is still the same. Instead of dealing with centers, theorists are now talking about larger brain systems. For example, in a recent article Magoun (1969) refers to the temporal lobe as "Penfield's brain," the reticular activating system as "Magoun's brain," the motor cortex and the association areas as "Pavlov's brain," and the medial forebrain bundle and related limbic structures as "Old's brain." Similarly, in discussing how these "systems" can be innervated by electrical or chemical means, Delgado (1966) uses the following analogy: "The role of electrical stimulation can be compared with that of the officer who pushes a button to launch a man into space. The officer is the essential, initial cause, but he is not responsible for the sequences, organization or planning of the tremendous complexity of mechanisms involved. Likewise, electrical stimulation starts a chain reaction in which the final result depends more on the structure of the components than on the trigger." Although Delgado acknowledges the complexity of the brain system, he is still assuming a fixed system or circuitry for aggression.

Contemporary textbooks provide accounts of various "triggering" phenomena using implanted electrodes. For example, it is stated that stimulation of the hypothalamus appears to have produced behaviors associated with primary drives, such as feeding, drinking, and sexual and maternal behavior. However, while these experiments are replicable, recent evidence indicates that electrical stimulation of discrete hypothalamic loci results in behavior patterns which are hardly as fixed as previously indicated. A specific site which is discovered always to elicit *feeding* when stimulated can be induced to "trigger" *drinking* if the food is removed. Similarly, stimulating of a "drinking site" will result in eating if water is removed. Animals were found to be as likely to eat food, gnaw on a dish, or drink water from stimulation of a single site from which a single exclusive behavior was originally elicited (Valenstein, Cox, & Kakolewski, 1968a, 1968b, 1969a, 1969b, 1970). The removal of the initially preferred stimulus results in a new behavior even though the parameters of stimulation and site of stimulation are unchanged. Recent evidence indicates that removal of the initially preferred stimulus is not even necessary. Repeated daily testing with both food and water present results in a shift from originally elicited drinking or originally elicited eating to a combination of eating and drinking (Milgram, Devor, & Server, 1971).

The fact that most other experiments involving electrical stimulation of the brain have been of short duration may have contributed to the failure to observe this multiplicity of function. The effects of environmental factors as well as repeated long-term stimulation have largely been overlooked. While the shortness of duration of electrical stimulation is understandable in situations involving human patients (Penfield, 1969), meaningful data can only be obtained when stimulation is carried out over protracted periods. It is of interest to report that Penfield's procedure was repeated using implanted electrodes (Mahl, Rothenberg, Delgado, & Hamlin, 1964). Stimulation of the associative cortex was repeated over a period of weeks. The events remembered were not fixed, but varied. The setting prior to and during electrical stimulation determined to a great extent what the patient recalled. Here we have a case where different sets of memories were produced by the same electrode placement and stimulus parameters.

Attempts to study the interrelations of brain and aggression, which is the main concern of this paper, provide further examples which are often cited as proof of a localization doctrine. We are all now familiar with accounts of how radio stimulation of the brain is used to stop a charging bull abruptly. The literature contains an overwhelming number of reports describing chemically- and electrically-evoked aggression in various species. However, it has been known for over a decade (Holst & St. Paul, 1962) that the pattern evoked was dependent on environmental influences. More recently Delgado and Mir (1969) found that radio stimulation evoked fighting as well as gestures correlated with aggression depending on which colony members were present. Once again, as was the case for feeding and memory, specification of the location of the electrode and the stimulus parameters alone did not provide a sufficient account. In view of these examples of multiplicity of functioning, one has to question the value of the concept of localization of behavior patterns.

Looking for brain centers for aggression makes about as much sense as looking for a brain center for the concept "person." While the concept of "person" is very useful at one level of analysis, it is doubtful that it could be useful at the brain level. The concept of aggression, while useful at some levels of analysis, may not be useful at the neurophysiological level. The wide range of forms which aggression can take supports this contention. Punching a guy in the mouth isn't the same as dropping napalm. I would simply suggest that the solution to the problem of aggression may well not be found in the brain and nervous system alone.

The point to be stressed is that perhaps too much emphasis has been placed on the search for invariant properties of neural-behavioral correlates and too little on their variability. Merely to describe what behavior pattern is correlated with stimulation of a particular brain area is insufficient. How the stimulation and behavior came to be correlated is what must be investigated. The examples just cited demonstrate that such an inquiry necessitates consideration of the history of the organism as well as external and internal factors and their effects over time.

The approach being advocated precludes statements to the effect that humans and other animals enter life endowed with genetically determined and highly specific neural circuits—that is, pre-wired. Proponents of a pre-wired theory often cite the work of Hubel and Wiesel (1963) which demonstrated that in the cat the neural circuitry between the retina and the occipital cortex exists at birth, before the eyes are open. These investigators carried their studies further however, and examined the possibility that the age of the subject or environmental inputs might be relevant factors. The functional connections present at birth were disrupted in an eye if it was deprived of patterned stimulation by occlusion during the first three months of life. When deprivation was instituted in adult cats or kittens more than three months of age, no functional deficits were observed (Weisel & Hubel, 1963a, 1963b). Following deprivation, the receptive fields of single neurons in the cortex were found to be altered and the cortical cells receiving binocular input were greatly reduced in number (Ganz, Fitch, & Satterberg, 1968; Weisel & Hubel, 1965a, 1965b). Additional evidence that input into sensory organs is necessary for the development of neural organization typically observed in the adult has been reviewed by Riesen (1966).

Often cited as strong evidence for a genetically determined wired-in system is the demonstration that fibers regenerating from the ganglion layer of the retina towards the brain of the adult frog ultimately arrive at the optic tectum in the ordered arrangement of terminals necessary for recovery of vision (Attardi & Sperry, 1963). This is truly amazing in view of the fact that at the point of optic nerve severance the growing fibers passed through the scarred tissue in random fashion. With visual sensitivity reestablished following nerve severance and rotation of the eye 180°, the visual field is inverted and reversed. In behavioral tests visual and motor responses were correspondingly displaced. A downward thrust was made in response to food placed above the head. Furthermore, there was no indication that the subject could ever adjust to the reversed visual field. (Sperry, 1951).

While these results are indeed impressive, the problem of exactly how the axon finds its way through the tissue and the mechanism of specificity of connection are still unresolved. Matters are not clarified by merely stating that the fibers are guided by a genetically determined biochemical code which creates a chemoaffinity. Whether these findings are generalizable to all species, stages of development, and types of neural tissues is also doubtful. Stone (1944, 1948), working with amphibian embryos which had their eyes grafted and rotated prior to the onset of vision, replicated these findings. Visual-motor disorientation was exhibited by the subjects throughout life. However, there are some important failures to replicate. Stone reported that the effect is obtained only if the young embryo eye is rotated *after* the late tail-bud stage. If the operation is carried out *prior* to this stage, normal vision results. That is, specificity of neuronal connections is not observed until a certain developmental stage has been attained. Similar results are reported by Jacobson (1967, 1969), who studied neuronal connectivity from an ontogenetic point of view. Species comparisons regarding the ability to adjust to visual field displacements have revealed that man and nonhuman primates do extremely well. Specific differences in the ability to adjust have been reported by Szantagothai (see Gaze & Watson, 1968) between the larval amphibia *Triturus vulgarus,* which does not adjust, and *Triturus cris-tatus,* which does.

A second limitation of the research supporting pre-wiring has been that it has been done on the long fi-ber systems, such as the optic tract. Although long axoned fibers are more accessible, they are far out-numbered by the shorter axoned interneurons. Ac-cording to Sperry (1971), these short interneurons, which he refers to as Cajal type II neurons, are still plastic in man beyond the age of twelve years. Be-cause of their plasticity these cells may yield interest-ing clues about behavior.

To summarize, while Sperry's work appears to support pre-wiring, it actually does not constitute strong evidence because it does not hold up across species, ontogenetic stages, and fiber types.

Let us review the major themes of this paper; first, when people look out on the world and observe that aggression is a major social problem, all too often they look to the brain for a solution. They seem to think they are getting down to the real thing, the real 'nitty gritty.' They also tend to look to other species, thinking that aggression in man can be accounted for in the same way as it can be in other animals. I have tried to show that these approaches to aggression and the solutions implied by them are scientifically un-sound. The major shortcoming has been improper generalization of specific experimental findings to ag-gression in humans. In their zeal to utilize scientific findings, people generalize carelessly across species and stages of development. To satisfactorily account for aggression many levels of analysis must be uti-lized. For example, first consider two dogs fighting

and, second, consider soldiers in a helicopter shooting into a rice paddy. Both may be called instances of
aggression. However, different levels of analysis will
have to be used to explain each case because each
represents the outcome of different levels of developmental integration (Schneirla, 1949, 1953, 1957). In
the case of the two dogs, pheromonal influences
(chemical signals) would have to be considered,
while pheromones would not be involved in the helicopter shooting. On the other hand, language and
political factors are probably of importance to the
soldiers, but certainly not to the dogs. Each instance
of aggression has to be analyzed and explained in appropriate terms and concepts.

REFERENCES

Attardi, G., and Sperry, R.W. Preferential selection
of central pathways by regenerating optic fibers. *Exp.
Neurol.*, 1963, 7: 46-64.

Brown, J.S. Problems presented by the concept of
acquired drives. In *Current theory and research in
motivation*. Lincoln, Nebraska: University of Nebraska Press, 1953.

Delgado, J.M.R. *Emotions.* Dubuque, Iowa: W.C.
Brown, 1966.

Delgado, J.M.R., and Mir, D. Fragmental organization of emotional behavior in the monkey. *Ann.
N.Y. Acad. Sci.*, 1969, *159*:731-751.

Ganz, L., Fitch, M., and Satterberg, J. The selective
effect of deprivation on receptive field shape determined neurophysiologically. *Exp. Neurol.*, 1968, *22:*

614-637.

Gaze, R.M., and Watson, W.E. Cell division and migration in the brain after optic nerve lesions. In G. E. W. Wolstenholme and M. O'Connor (Eds.), *Growth of the nervous system*. Boston: Little, Brown, 1968.

Heath, R.G. Electrical self-stimulation of the brain in man. *Amer. J. Psychiat.*, 1963, *120*:571-577.

Heath, R.G. (Ed.). *The role of pleasure in behavior*. New York: Hoeber, 1964.

Hebb, C.O. Drives and the C.N.S. (conceptual nervous system). *Psychol. Rev.*, 1955, *62*:243-254.

Holst, E. von, and St. Paul, U. von. Electrically controlled behavior. *Sci. Amer.*, 1962, *206*:50-59.

Hubel, D.H., and Wiesel, T.N. Receptive fields of cells in striate cortex of very young, visually inexperienced kittens. *J. Neurophysiol.*, 1963, *26*:994-1002.

Jacobson, M. Retinal ganglion cells: Specification of central connections in larval Xenopus laevis. *Science*, 1967, *155*:1106-1108.

Jacobson, M. Development of specific neuronal connections. *Science*, 1969, *163*:543-547.

Lindsley, D.B. Emotion. In S.S. Stevens (Ed.), *Handbook of experimental psychology*. New York: Wiley, 1951.

Lorenz, K. *On aggression*. New York: Harcourt, Brace and World, 1966.

McDougall, W. *An introduction to social psychology*. (14th ed.) New York: Barnes and Noble, 1960.

Magoun, H.W. The ascending reticular activating system. *Res. Publ. Ass. Nerv. Ment. Dis.*, 1952, *30*:480-492.

Magoun, H.W. Advances in brain research with

implications for learning. In K. H. Pribram (Ed.), *On the biology of learning.* New York: Harcourt, Brace, & World, 1969.

Mahl, G.E., Rothenberg, A., Delgado, J.M.R., and Hamlin, H. Psychological responses in the human to intracerebral electrical stimulation. *Psychosom. Med.* 1964, *26*:337-368.

Mark, V.H., and Ervin, F. R. *Violence and the brain.* New York: Harper & Row, 1970.

Mark, V.H., Ervin, F.R., Sweet, W.H., and Delgado, J.M.R. Remote telemeter stimulation and recording from implanted temporal lobe electrodes. *Confin. Neurol.,* 1969, *31*:86-93.

Milgram, N.W., Devor, M., and Server, A.C. Spontaneous changes in behavior induced by electrical stimulation of the lateral hypothalamus in rats. *J. Comp. Physiol. Psychol.,* 1971, *75*:491-499.

Penfield, W. Consciousness, memory, and man's conditioned reflexes. In K. H. Pribram (Ed.), *On the biology of learning.* New York: Harcourt, Brace, & World, 1969.

Riesen, S.H. Sensory deprivation. In E. Stellar & J. Sprague (Eds.), *Progress in physiological psychology.* Vol. 1, New York: Academic Press, 1966.

Schneirla, T.C. Levels in the psychological capacities of animals. In R.W. Sellars, V.J. McGill, and M. Farber (Eds.), *Philosophy for the future.* New York: Macmillan, 1949.

Schneirla, T.C. The concept of levels in the study of social phenomena. In M. Sherif & C. Sherif, (Eds.), *Groups in harmony and tension.* New York: Harper, 1953.

Schneirla, T.C. The concept of development in

comparative psychology. In D.B. Harris (Ed.), *The concept of development.* Univ. Minn. Press, Minneapolis: 1957.

Sperry, R.W. Mechanisms of neural maturation. In S. S. Stevens (Ed.), *Handbook of experimental psychology.* New York: Wiley, 1951.

Sperry, R.W. How a developing brain gets itself properly wired for adaptive function. In E. Tobach, L.R. Aronson, and E. Shaw, (Eds.), *The biopsychology of development.* New York: Academic Press, 1971.

Stone, L.S. Functional polarization in retinal development and its reestablishment in regeneratory retinae of rotated grafted eyes. *Proc. Soc. Exper. Biol. & Med.* 1944, *57*:13-14.

Stone, L.S. Functional polarization in developing and regenerating retinae of transplanted eyes. *Ann. N.Y. Acad. Sci.,* 1948, *49*:856-865.

Valenstein, E.S., Cox, V.C., and Kakolewski, J.W. Modification of motivated behavior elicited by electrical stimulation of the hypothalamus. *Science,* 1968, *159*:1119-1121. (a)

Valenstein, E.S., Cox, V.C., and Kakolewski, J.W. The motivation underlying eating elicited by lateral hypothalamic stimulation. *Physiol. Behav.,* 1968, *3*:969-971.(b)

Valenstein, E.S., Cox, V.C., and Kakolewski, J.W. Hypothalamic motivational systems: Fixed or plastic neural circuits? *Science,* 1969, *163*:1084.(a)

Valenstein, E.S., Cox, V.C., and Kakolewski, J.W. 1969b. The hypothalamus and motivational behavior. In J.T. Tapp (Ed.), *Reinforcement and behavior.* New York: Academic Press, 1969.(b)

Valenstein, E.S., Cox, V.C., and Kakolewski, J.W. Reexamination of the role of the hypothalamus in motivation. *Psychol. Rev., 1970,* 77:16-31.

Wiesel, T.N., and Hubel, D.H. Effects of visual deprivation on morphology and physiology of cells in the cat's lateral geniculate body. *J. Neurophysiol.,* 1963, *26*:978-993.(a)

Wiesel, T.N., and Hubel, D.H. Single-cell responses in striate cortex of kittens deprived of vision in one eye. *J. Neurophysiol.,* 1963, *26*:1003-1017.(b)

Wiesel, T.N., and Hubel, D.H. Comparison of the effects of unilateral and bilateral eye closure on cortical unit responses in kittens. *J. Neurophysiol.,* 1965, *28*:1029-1040.(a)

Wiesel, T.N., and Hubel, D.H. Extent of recovery from the effects of visual deprivation in kittens. *J. Neurophysiol.,* 1965, *28*:1060-1072.(b)

*Social Darwinism
Rides Again*

Ethel Tobach

I wish to thank Howard Topoff whose comments were most helpful in the course of preparation of this manuscript. He is, of course, not accountable for its contents.

The concept of Social Darwinism[1] had its explicit beginning in the evolutionary thought of Spencer (1910). His phrase "survival of the fittest" referred to cultures, but was adopted by Darwin to explicate the process of natural selection. Darwin (1904), used the phrase in relation to the transmission of adaptive characteristics through reproduction. The amalgamation of Spencer's concept with Darwin's theory of the evolution of species produced a seemingly scientific rationalization for the 19th century European and American view of the peoples of the world as two populations, one of which was superior to the other by reason of physical and mental characteristics (Pearson, 1892). This rationalization came to be known as Social Darwinism (Harris, 1968; Hofstadter, 1955).

The history of these two concepts exemplifies the ever-present complexity of the relationship between the scientist as a member of society and as an investigator of natural phenomena. Some scientists believe that scientific labor in its conceptualization, execu-

[1]For a discussion of another phrase to describe the concept of Social Darwinism, or "biocultural theory" or "Biological Spencerism" as Harris terms it, see Harris (1968) and Carneiro (1967).

tion, and products is independent of the societal setting in which it is done. It is becoming clear to a growing number of scientists that this is an illusion (Eisenberg, 1972; Loebl, 1971; Mellanby, 1971; Price, 1971; Rabinowitch, 1971; Ravetz, 1971; Rose & Rose, 1971; Siekevitz, 1972; Stark, 1972; Szent-Gyorgyi, 1971), although the historian has long been aware of this (Kevles, 1970). The scientist has little protection against societal forces that determine not only the kind of research to be supported, but the uses to which the results of such research are to be put (Galston, 1970). There have always been and will continue to be scientists whose value systems are consonant with those of the social institutions that make such decisions (Cattell, 1910; Galton, 1892; Pearson, 1892).

Since the development of Social Darwinism, the concept of active human intervention in the evolutionary process of natural selection has been adopted by many biologists, psychologists, and sociologists. They have organized actively to promote programs for social action based on eugenic principles designed to "improve the human species." These organizations and scientists have had audiences of differing size and character through the years (see, for example, the following periodicals: *Biology and Human Affairs; Eugenics Review; Eugenics Society Symposia; Mankind Quarterly; Race*). Today there is an increase in the visibility and apparently in the popularity of these theories about the improvement of our national quality (Chase, 1972; Herrnstein, 1971; Ingle, 1964, 1971; Naroll, 1970; National Academy of Sciences, 1972). Some attribute the widespread concern among scientists to the significant advances in molecular biology and the prospects of genetic engineering (Gaylin, 1972; Nagle, 1971). An analysis needs to be made of a possible relationship between these significant developments in genetics and the stage of historical development of the world. For example, Watson (1968) points out that the discovery of the genetic code was made possible by the advanced technology which became available to biologists. Others have pointed out that much of the support for basic science has been the result of the international conflicts between differing socio-economic-political systems. These conflicts, which lead to war as well as an emphasis on improved technology, also lead to an intensification of conflict between peoples and classes. A notable result of this most recent development in world history has been the emergence of new national states that have in turn had an effect on the people of previous colonial powers. The United States and England are outstanding examples of this. But, the complex and continuing crises as evidenced by intensification of racial conflict, unemployment, educational failures, and drug abuse in society in the United States today cannot be ignored and thought irrelevant to the present prominence of Social Darwinistic thinking.

Social Darwinism arose during the most active period of industrialization and developing colonialism. The issue was the weeding out of the weak, the ill, the poor, the "socially unfit" (Galton, 1892; Malthus, 1817; Pearson, 1892). The "survival of the fittest" was an appropriate concept for that goal. As colonialism became dominant during the early part of the 20th century, genetic superiority was formulated in ethnic, national, and "racial" terms (Grant, 1916). Today the discussion of genetic fitness in the United States is taking place in a time of national economic disturbance when limited national resources have to be assigned to the training of a skilled work force necessary to maintain an idealized style of life.

The concepts of Social Darwinism have been criticized (Harris, 1968; Hofstadter, 1955) but the underlying assumptions purported to be the scientific basis of Social Darwinism need to be analyzed. Although such an analysis will do little to combat the prejudicial discrimination practiced against various ethnic populations, it is essential that scientists themselves examine the scientific validity of the concept. They may then want to examine the interpretations made of their own work in support of Social Darwinism and the uses to which their experimental results are put. This is particularly necessary for the geneticist, the ethologist, the psychologist, and for the behavior geneticist.

THE ASSUMPTIONS UNDERLYING SOCIAL DARWINISM

Three assumptions underlying Social Darwinism need to be explicitly stated and analyzed:

A. The evolutionary processes of speciation and survival apply to human beings not only in regard to their categorization as biological organisms, but in regard to their behavior, including socialization and cultural institutions.

B. Behavior is determined by genetic processes; the

environment is seen as dichotomously contradictory to heredity. (Kahn, 1970; Wolanski, 1970).

C. All societies, including human society, are stratified in terms of power and dominance and these stratifications are determined by genetic processes.

A. *The evolutionary processes of speciation and survival apply to human beings not only in regard to their categorization as biological organisms, but in regard to their behavior, including socialization and cultural institutions.*

Contemporary proponents of the view that natural selection operates to eliminate ethnic groups or "races" and cultures find support in the writings of Lorenz (1965), who has not addressed himself to issues of racial fitness since the 1940's (Eisenberg, 1972); in those of Skinner (1966), who states that contingency reinforcement operates to eliminate species as well as to modify individual behavior within the limits of individual genetic endowment; and in Jensen (1971a), who writes that the laws that govern the intellectual, social, and moral fitness of human beings are the same as those that govern the evolutionary fitness of species. Jensen's works will be discussed later. He has expressed agreement (Jensen, 1971b) with Herrnstein, whose writing is analyzed in relation to Social Darwinism below.

The critiques of Lorenzian ethology are well-known and available (Callan, 1970; Lehrman, 1970; Schneirla, 1970a, 1970b). In the Lorenzian theory of the evolution of behavior, three postulates are particularly acceptable to the Social Darwinists who today are the spokesmen for modern eugenics. The first

of these is the assumption that all behavior is programmed in evolution. The second is the concept
that some behavior patterns have persisted because of
their adaptive values. According to this behavior theory, changes in society that inhibit the relationships
between these patterns and "the natural world" will
lead to abnormal individual and group behavior.
The example given by Lorenz and some of his fol-
lowers is the deterioration of racial stock through
domestication; in the case of the human, through ur-
banization. Thirdly, through rituals designed to
channel instinctive behavior, it should be possible to
counteract these negative effects on adaptive, inherited behavior patterns. One of these inherited behavior patterns in the Lorenzian system is that of associative mating which has evolved to promote the
survival of the species. The eugenicists use these concepts to bolster their assertion that the middle and
upper classes, which have been most constructive in
preserving the quality of the human species, need to
be educated in this theory to encourage them to reproduce in numbers.[2]

The psychological, historical-philosophical, and
socio-political aspects of Skinner's theory have been

[2]The following is an Editorial Comment: "Top People have
Larger Families," from *Eugenics Review*, 1967 (59:1):

"Two contributions in this issue of the Review throw an en-
couraging light on the aims and activities of the Society. First on
pages 46-48, it is shown that scholars at Winchester College are
not only replacing themselves, in the most recent generations,
but are also increasing their kind. In the process they are doing
better than the population at large. Secondly, pages 70-72 give a
first look at the 1961 Census fertility data for England and Wales,

criticized (Black, 1972; Chomsky, 1971; Kantor, 1970; Toynbee, 1972; Washburn, 1968) and these are not directly pertinent to the issue here.

Skinner's plan (1948) for behavioral modification is designed to assure the survival of the culture in which his techniques are employed. He has indicated that the goal of survival suggests competition with other cultures as in Social Darwinism and has rejected aggression as a contingency for survival, substituting cooperative behavior (Skinner, 1972a). He does not modify his original position, however, and continues to view the processes of cultural development and change as being the same as those that bring about speciation and species survival.

In Skinner's theory, the environment includes the genes. The environment, however, determines the genetic endowment of the individual. He says this comes about through natural selection which operates in the way reinforcement contingencies operate in determining individual behavior. Throughout his formulation, the genetic contribution is seen as a given, limiting potential that governs the condi-

with special reference to the differentials between socio-economic groups; they indicate that, among white-collar workers, people with the most intellectually-demanding jobs are now having the largest families. Moreover, in their fertility, unskilled manual workers now differ less from other types of wage-earner than they did.

These trends are beneficial to the nation as a whole; in a competitive world the best possible quality of thought and action is needed, and in a technology of ever-growing complexity there is a need for an increasing supply of capable people so that progress can be maintained.''

tionability of the species and the individual. This concept differs in no significant way from Lorenz's proposition that the potential for modification is fixed and predetermined as are the characteristics of the species and the individual. This static view of the biochemical process in the developmental experience of the individual ignores the widely-held fundamental conceptualization of the genetic process as seen by geneticists (Herskowitz, 1965), developmental geneticists (Gluecksohn-Waelsch, 1951), and others (Tobach, 1972; Topoff, this volume). The biochemical entity called a "gene" is inseparable from the circumstances in which it is situated at all times in its viable history. It cannot function at any time independently of the milieu in which it acts and which acts upon it to bring about a fusion of the two processes. This fusion is expressed in other biochemical functions from which structures are derived and from which more complex, higher integrative levels of function are derived, such as physiological processes and organismic behavior.

This lack of precision about genetic processes is further reflected in Skinner's view of contingency acting to bring about the adaptation and survival of the species as being similar to the contingencies which in his theory control behavior and the adjustment of the individual (cf Jensen). This is the same analysis offered by the Social Darwinists when they see natural selection functioning to permit species to survive and, in the same way, to permit cultures to survive.

What is a more accurately formulated relationship among the three processes: evolutionary speciation, development of individual differences, and the his-

torical development of different cultures? It is clear
that generalizations must account for the differences
as well as for the similarities of these phenomena.

Although natural selection is an evolutionary process that applies to all forms of living matter, its
most frequent application is to species or other taxonomic categories (see Topoff, this volume). Within
any species, however, variations among individuals
come about by many different processes. An important factor in such processes is the nature of the relationship of the organism to its environment. Given
a species that is more capable of control and selection
of the environment than another species, the first species is likely to show more variation among the individual members than is the second species.

In the case of human beings, the processes that determine the selection and control of environmental
factors have reached a complexity and level of organization and integration that is not seen anywhere
else in the animal world. This new level of integration of structure, function, and developmental experience is characterized by such significant differences
from other animals as language, culture, and work
relationships—all part of societal processes that pro-
foundly affect each individual human being as well
as groups of humans. These societal processes involve the communication of ideas and interpersonal
relationships that determine the historical development of societies and cultures.

Natural selection did not bring about the abolition
of slavery. Environmental factors like geography and
climate play a fundamental role in natural selection.
It was not an interaction with environmental factors

(geophysical, climatic, or pathologic epidemiological agents) that eliminated slave populations. Slavery was abolished in many places because of historic processes having to do with ideas that arose out of changing relationships among people and between people and their environment (industrialization, technological advances, etc.)

It might be argued by some Social Darwinists that the abolition of slavery was nonetheless part of the human evolutionary process, for by freeing the slaves, they were placed in the open competitive industrial society in which "bad" genes would be eliminated and "good" genes would be able to survive, enabling the individuals who had them to rise to successful positions in society (Herrnstein, 1971). However, according to this same viewpoint, in all populations (usually defined in terms of "race") there are "good" and "bad" genes. The process of natural selection for "good" and "bad" genes as exemplified in the cultural institution of slavery would have to operate very quickly in view of the fact that peoples who have been slave-holders have become slaves in one generation, and vice versa.

These complicated considerations are examples of the difficulties encountered in the extrapolation of principles from the functioning of nonhuman species to human beings. In the case of human beings, change in societal forms and relationships is dependent upon processes that are many steps removed from the biochemical process by which structure and function of organismic systems and organs are brought about. The error in the first assumption underlying Social Darwinism is the reductionistic approach to natural phenomena that results in the dismissal of species differences.

Just as one cannot use principles governing ionic equilibrium at the membrane of a neurone to explain reproductive behavior in an animal, one cannot explain cultural institutions by understanding the biochemical processes of individual development. Circulating levels of hormones significantly affect neuronal function, and thus affect reproductive behavior. But knowing how neurones function is not sufficient to understand the change in response by one bird to another at a particular time of the year in a given situation, i.e., the explanation cannot be made in terms of ionic equilibrium, or by other reductionistic analyses.

Reducing the societal processes that relate to cultural change to the processes of natural selection that operate in speciation cannot explain those societal processes.

B. *Behavior is determined by genetic processes; the environment is seen as dichotomously contradictory to heredity.*

In Skinner's *Walden Two* (1948), individual differences in I.Q. and physical prowess are accepted as natural limitations on the roles assumed by individuals. The implicit assumption is made that having kept the environment constant for all, with no competition or comparison among individuals, the inherited characteristics of the individual will determine his or her work category (cf Herrnstein, 1971). This conceptualization of heritability is dealt with in the paper by Topoff in this volume.

Jensen (1970) views heritability in much the same way as Skinner and the relation between this view of behavior and class and "race" are made explicit in many of his papers (Jensen, 1968, 1971c). Jensen repeats his concern for the function of the individual child in many of these papers, but in his formulation of an approach to teaching the individual, he cites the results of his work with groups and populations of individuals to support his thesis about the inheritance of intelligence. This type of logic has been described and criticized by Hirsch (1970) and others as "typological."

Characteristics of populations of animals and plants are determined through careful investigation of the frequencies of certain characteristics of populations in different generations. These frequencies of given characteristics, such as type of fur or hair, or size of leaves and petal color, can then be said to be typical of a population. One can discuss the frequencies of their occurrence on the basis of these calculations. In no case do these statistical statements give any information about the characteristics of an individual, or how the individual's characteristics came about. To do so would require an analysis of the functioning of the biochemical systems (including genes) and the developmental history of the individual which would also include the physical and social characteristics of the milieu in which that development took place.

Inferences about mechanisms of adaptation and selection pressures for species are not always useful in predicting or understanding an individual organism's response to situations that threaten its survi-

val; the individual response pattern may be nonadjustive for the individual, although for the species
the behavioral response may have been adaptive (Tobach, Adler, & Adler, 1973). For example, the period-
ic population fluctuation in lemmings is adaptive for
the survival of the species but nonadjustive for the
individual.

Much of Jensen's discussion about the phylogeny
and ontogeny of intelligence is based upon a comparison of species in regard to their performance in
equivalent tasks. As Maier and Schneirla (1964) and
Warden, Jenkins, and Warner (1934) pointed out in
texts that have been basic reading for students of the
evolution of behavior, the concept of "intelligence"
for nonhuman animals has low utility. It is impossible to arrive at a comparable scale of "intelligence"
for a series of animal species on the basis of performance on a series of tasks that are hopefully graded
in difficulty. Depending on the species, the same task
can be "difficult" or "simple." This may come about
because the sensory stimuli and motor responses re-
quired in the tasks cannot be equated for different
species. It should be noted that differences in performance and learning by different *species* is being discussed. To equate differences among species in this
regard with differences in different populations of a
single species, such as human beings, is another example of typological thinking.

To stress that genetics is not the determining factor
in behavior is not to deny the participation of biochemical processes in the development, growth, and
maturation of individual organisms. Behavior is an
integration of the function of all levels of organismic

organization, including the biochemical activities carried on by the genes, during the history of the organism in which all experiences are continuously being integrated. Experience includes all effective stimuli and their trace effects (Schneirla, 1970c).

Human behavior is significantly different from that of all other animals, including other primates, in that the socialization process leads to an inseparable relationship between the individual person and society. By virtue of societal factors, the very conditions under which the human is conceived, the course of gestation and parturition, and of development, growth, and maturation are in effect societally determined. The development of thinking processes, the interrelationships among human beings, and the effect of societal factors on physiological function throughout life are all a function of the socialization process without which human survival is impossible. For these reasons awareness of one's ethnicity, class position, or sex plays a powerful role in behavior and performance. (Katz, 1968; Ledvinka, 1971; Tobach, 1971; Vroman, 1970).

C. *All societies, including human society, are stratified in terms of power and dominance and these stratifications are determined by genetic processes.*

The beliefs of the early Social Darwinists about the stratification of society have never been completely abandoned within the scientific community (see Eugenics Review; Tiger, 1970) although the formulations may change. Some contemporary ethologists and psychologists now support this thesis by making the generalization that there has always been class stratification accompanied by the existence of one class that maintains power by virtue of possession of the instruments of power in human societies which are but an extension of the dominance hierarchies found in nonhuman animal social organizations. It has been pointed out by anthropologists that not all human cultures have these characteristics (Leacock, 1967) and that where there is stratification the indicators of dominance vary from culture to culture.

The early Social Darwinists were most concerned about the existence of the poverty-stricken, a condition that they attributed to genetic factors. In complex technological societies, the characteristics of the unemployed vary with the historical era in which they are being examined. Thus, during the 1930's in the United States, the characteristics of the unemployed were those of every subpopulation in the nation, although the frequency of unemployed varied according to ethnic and sex variables. During more recent days, when the aeronautic and allied industries as well as academic and research institutions have released vast numbers of engineers, Ph.D.'s, and technicians, the characteristics of the unemployed resemble the characteristics of the dominant sector of society in the United States, i.e., white, male, non-Catholic, and non-Jewish (see also King, 1973).

The Social Darwinist accepts the concept that unemployment is a temporary phenomenon in our society and is concerned with the "unemployables" who do not work even during periods of prosperity. The concept that employment is a function of societal processes is dismissed and the solution to the problem is sought in family allowances (Fisher, 1968) to encourage the middle class to reproduce rather than the lower classes in which most of the unemployed are usually found.

Herrnstein (1971) believes that individuals with "adaptive genes" are able to move out of lower classes to higher classes. Those who do not have the adaptive genes are presumably condemned to a marginal existence which may remove them from the population that reproduces successfully. Herrnstein makes no explicit statement about the fate of this marginal subpopulation. Others have been more active in stating their solutions.[3] The recent developments in molecular biology have interested scientists in general in this aspect of Social Darwinism and some are attempting to derive democratic procedures to be followed in genetic engineering for the future. (Verhoog, 1971).

In Skinner's view, society is stratified and dependent ultimately on the genetic endowment of individuals. In his original view of the society based on pos-

[3]See Chase (1972) for an excellent contribution to the history of these notions. The following is from Shockley (1971):

"The First Amendment makes it safe for us in the United States to try to find humane eugenic measures. As a step in such search, I propose as a *thinking exercise* a voluntary, sterilization bonus plan.

Bonuses will be offered for sterilization. Income tax-payers get nothing. Bonuses for all others, regardless of sex, race, or welfare status, would depend on best scientific estimates of hereditary factors in disadvantages such as diabetes, epilepsy, heroin addiction, arthritis, etc. At a bonus rate of $1,000 for each point below 100 IQ, $30,000 put in trust for a 70 IQ moron of twenty-child potential might return $250,000 to tax-payers in reduced costs of men-

itive reinforcement (control and countercontrol), the limits set by I.Q. and physical prowess determine the role of the individual. He has indicated that he has modified his original scheme and would now include a behavioral engineer who would be able, by analysis of the individuals, to make judgments about the appropriate reinforcements to be used (Skinner, 1972b). One may assume that the same I.Q. limitations will determine who can assume that role.

Skinner's book (1971) ends on a utopian note of optimism in projecting a world without violence or poverty. The examples of individuals who would need control seem rather benign: children, retardates, and psychotics. But all three categories have been based on changing criteria, depending upon laws, social practices, and the value systems of the controlling agents in societies. In Skinner's books and statements he is always careful to point out that he is not proposing any mechanism or value system for determining who sets these criteria.

SOCIETAL FACTORS IN THE RESURGENCE OF SOCIAL DARWINISM

In an essay entitled "Science Can Never Be Retrograde," Gerard Piel (1972) calls upon biologists to

tal retardation care. Ten percent of the bonus in spot cash might put our national talent for entrepreneurship into action.

A motivation boost might be to permit those sterilized to be employed at below minimum standard wages without any loss of a welfare floor income. Could this provide opportunity for those now unemployable?"

contribute to the solution of society's crises. The public is doing the same, possibly because they have given financial and other resources to the scientist for a generation. They are indeed being offered answers to their problems by geneticists, evolutionary biologists, and behavioral scientists. All of the answers, however, appear to be based on zoomorphism: a reductionistic approach in which the human species is made equivalent to other animals. Coupled with a pervading and growing distrust of science and its apparent effects on the quality of life, this approach is meeting with an apparent widespread welcome by the public.

One possible explanation for the promulgation and acceptance of these ideas underlying Social Darwinism may be that the zoomorphic approach, after all, is based on the notion of a predetermined destiny about which society can do little. In the face of changing international, ethnic, and technological-human relationships, these ideas present the least challenge to the status quo. This leads to the perpetuation and resurgence of such ideas as Social Darwinism. These and other possibilities should be discussed by all sectors of society; the scientist cannot be omitted from that discussion.

Addendum

I think the reader will find the following two references of interest. One is an article entitled, "Apes and Original Sin," by Sally Binford which appeared in *Human Behavior* in the November/December 1972 issue. In that article she also talks about an important book: *The Human Imperative* by Alexander Alland, Jr.

In addition, a third event has taken place in the scientific community which is worthy of note. Leon J. Kamin has done a masterful job of bringing together the history of the testing and eugenics movement in the psychological profession since the days of Binet. Dr. Kamin is preparing a manuscript based on the seminars and colloquia he has been giving recently at various universities in the northeastern area of the United States, as well as at the Eastern Psychological Association meeting in 1973.

REFERENCES

Biology and Human Affairs. Published by The British Social Biology Council, London.

Birch, H.G., and Gussow, J.D. *Disadvantaged children: Health, nutrition and school failure.* New York: Harcourt, Brace and World, 1970.

Black, M.A. Disservice to all. *Center Report,* 1972, *5*(1): 53-57.

Callan, H. *Ethology and society.* Oxford: Clarendon Press, 1970.

Carneiro, R. Introduction to *The evolution of society: Selections from H. Spencer's Principles of Sociology.* University of Chicago Press, 1967: vii-ix.

Cattell, J. McK. A further statistical study of American men of science. *Science,* 1910, *32*(827):633-648.

Chase, A. *The biological imperatives.* New York: Afred A. Knopf, 1972.

Chomsky, N. The case against B.F. Skinner. *The New York Review*, December 30, 1971: 18-24.

Darwin, F. (Ed.). *The Life and Letters of Charles Darwin*. Vol. II. New York: D. Appleton and Company, 1904.

Ehrman, L., Omenn, G.S., and Caspari, E. *Genetics, environment and behavior*. New York: Academic Press, 1972.

Eisenberg, L. The *human* nature of human nature. *Science,* 1972, *176:*123-128.

Eugenics Review. Published by the Eugenics Society, London.

Eugenics Review. Top people have larger families. Editorial Comment. 1967, *59:* 1.

Eugenics Society Symposia. J.E. Meade and A.S. Parkes (Eds.). Published by the Eugenics Society, Edinburgh.

Fisher, R. A. Family allowances. *Eugenics Review,* 1938, *60*(2): 109-117.

Galston, A.W. Plants, people and politics. *Plant Science Bulletin,* 1970, *16*(1): 1-7.

Galton, F. *Hereditary Genius*. New York: Macmillan Co., 1892.

Gaylin, W. We have the awful knowledge to make exact copies of human beings. *The New York Times Magazine,* March 5, 1972.

Gluecksohn-Waelsch, S. Physiological genetics of the mouse. *Adv. in Genet.,* 1951, *4:* 2-49.

Grant, M. *The passing of the great race*. New York: Scribner's, 1916.

Halsey, A. H. *Sociology, biology and population control*. The Galton Lecture, 1967.

Harris, M. *The rise of anthropological theory.*

New York: Thomas Y. Crowell Co., 1968.

Herrnstein, R. I.Q. *The Atlantic,* 1971, *228*: 44-64.

Herskowitz, I. H. *Genetics.* (2nd ed.). Boston: Little, Brown and Co., 1965.

Hirsch, J. Behavior-genetic analysis and its biosocial consequences. *Semin. Psychiat.,* 1970, *2*:89-105.

Hofstadter, R. *Social Darwinism in American thought.* Boston: Beacon Press, 1955.

Ingle, D.J. Racial differences and the future. *Science,* 1964, *146*:375-379.

Ingle, D. J. Causality. *Perspect. Biol. & Med.,* 1971, *14*:410-423.

Jensen, A.R. Social class, race, and genetics: Implications for education. *Amer. Educat. Res. J.,* 1968, *5*(1): 1-42.

Jensen, A.R. The heritability of intelligence. *Engineering and Science,* 1970, *33*(6): 1-4.

Jensen, A.R. The phylogeny and ontogeny of intelligence. *Perspect. Biol. & Med.* 1971, *15*:37-43.(a)

Jensen, A.R. Letter to *Atlantic Monthly,* December, 1971.(b)

Jensen, A.R. Can we and should we study race differences? In *Race and intelligence.* Anthropological Studies Number 8. Washington, D.C.: American Anthropological Association, 1971.(c)

Kahn, R.M. Brief proposal: Both horns of a dilemma are usually attached to the same bull. *Perspect. Biol. Med.,* 1970, *13*(4):633-635.

Kantor, J.R. An analysis of the experimental analysis of behavior (TEAB). *J. Exp. Anal. Behav.,* 1970, *13*(1):101-108.

Katz, I. Some motivational determinants of racial differences in intellectual achievement. In *Science and the concept of race,* Margaret Mead, Theodosius Dobzhansky, Ethel Tobach, and Robert E. Light (Eds.). New York: Columbia University Press, 1968.

Kevles, D.J. "Into hostile political camps": The reorganization of international science in World War I. *Isis,* 1970, *62*(1):47-60.

King, J.C. Are we in danger of drowning in a sea of low I.Q.'s? 1973. Unpublished manuscript.

Leacock, E. B. Territoriality and aggression in animals and man. Proc. Pacem in Terris Institute, Manhattan College, New York, 1967.

Ledvinka, J.Race of interviewer and the language elaboration of black interviewees. *J. Social Issues,* 1971, *27*(4):185-197.

Lehrman, D. S. Semantic and conceptual issues in the nature-nurture problem. In *Development and evolution of behavior. Essays in memory of T.C. Schneirla.* L. R. Aronson, E. Tobach, J.S. Rosenblatt, and D.S. Lehrman (Eds.), San Francisco: W. H. Freeman Co., 1970: 17-52.

Loebl, E. Two views of the role of science. *The New York Times,* November 2, 1971.

Lorenz, K. *Evolution and modification of behavior.* Chicago: University of Chicago Press, 1965.

Maier, N. R. F., and Schneirla, T. C. *Principles of animal psychology.* New York: Dover Publications, 1964.

Malthus, T. R. *An essay on the principle of population.* London: J. Murray, 1817.

Mankind Quarterly. R. Gayre of Gayre, Ed. Edinburgh, Scotland (publ.)

Mellanby, K. Conflicts of loyalty in science. *Nature,* 1971, *234*:17-18.

Nagle, J. J. Genetic engineering. *Bull. Atomic Scientists*, 1971:43-45.

Naroll, R. Book review of *The evolution of society: Selections from Herbert Spencer's "Principles of Sociology."* *J. Hist. Behav. Sci.*, 1970, *6*(4):375-377.

National Academy of Sciences. Recommendations with respect to the behavioral and social aspects of human genetics. Ad Hoc Committee on Genetic Factors in Human Performance. *Proc. Nat. Acad. Sci.*, 1972, *69*(1):1-3.

Pearson, K. *The grammar of science.* London: Walter Scott, 1892 (Charles Scribner's Sons, New York).

Piel, G. *The acceleration of history.* New York: Alfred A. Knopf, 1972.

Price, T. Conflicts of loyalty in science. *Nature*, 1917, *234*:18.

Rabinowitch, E. Two views of the role of science. *The New York Times.* November 2, 1971.

Race. Published by the Institute of Race Relations, London.

Ravetz, J.R. Conflicts of loyalty in science. *Nature*, 1971, *234*:20.

Rose, S., and Rose, H. Social responsibility (III): The myth of the neutrality of science. *Impact of Sci. on Technology*, 1971, *21*(2):137-149.

Schneirla, T.C. Interrelationships of the "innate" and the "acquired" in instinctive behavior. In *Selected writings of T. C. Schneirla.* L. R. Aronson, E. Tobach, J. S. Rosenblatt, and D. S. Lehrman (Eds.), San Francisco: W. H. Freeman Co., 1970: 131-188 Part II.(a)

Schneirla, T. C. Instinct and aggression: Review of

Konrad Lorenz' *Evolution and modification of behavior* and *On aggression*. In *Selected writings of T. C. Schneirla*. San Francisco: W. H. Freeman Co., 1970: 192-196, Part II. (b)

Schneirla, T. C. Aspects of stimulation and organization in approach-withdrawal processes underlying vertebrate behavioral development. In *Selected writings of T. C. Schneirla*. San Francisco: W. H. Freeman Co., 1970: 344-412, Part IV.(c)

Shockley, W. Dysgenics—a social problem reality evaded by the illusion of infinite plasticity of human intelligence? Amer. Psychol. Assoc. Nat. Conv., September 7, 1971, Press Release.

Siekevitz, P. The social responsibility of scientists. *Ann. N. Y. Acad. Sci.*, 1972, *196*:197-291.

Skinner, B. F. *Walden two*. New York: The Macmillan Co., 1948.

Skinner, B. F. The phylogeny and ontogeny of behavior. *Science*, 1966, *153:* 1205-1213.

Skinner, B. F. *Beyond freedom and dignity*. New York: Alfred A. Knopf, 1971.

Skinner, B. F. Freedom and dignity revisited. *The New York Times*, August 11, 1972.(a)

Skinner, B. F. An interview with B. F. Skinner. *Center Report*, 1972, *5*(1):63-65.(b).

Spencer, H. *The principles of sociology*. Volumes I, II, and III. London and New York: D. Appleton & Co., 1910.

Stark, N. Commentary—Ecology and ethics. *Ecology*, 1972, *53*:1-2.

Szent-Gyorgyi, A. Science and government are inseparable. *The New York Times*, December 19, 1971.

Tiger, L. Dominance in human societies. *Ann. Rev. Ecol. System,* 1970, *1*:287-306.

Tobach, E. The meaning of the cryptanthroparion. In *Genetics, environment and behavior.* L. Ehrman, G. Omenn, and E. Caspari (Eds.), New York: Academic Press, 1972: 219-329.

Tobach, E. Some evolutionary aspects of human gender. *J. Orthopsychiat.,* 1971 *71*(5): 710-715.

Tobach, E., Adler, H. E., and Adler, L. L. Comparative psychology at issue. *Ann. N. Y. Acad. Sci.,* 1973 (in press).

Toynbee, A. An uneasy feeling of unreality. *Center Report,* 1972, *5*(1):58-62.

Verhoog, H. Review of *Fabricated man: The ethics of genetic control* by P. Ramsey. *Genetica,* 1971, *42*(4):480-482.

Vroman, G. Asian-Americans today, 1970. Unpublished manuscript.

Warden, C. J., Jenkins, T. N., and Warner, L. H. *Comparative psychology.* New York: The Ronald Press Company 1934.

Washburn, J. L. Political thought of B. F. Skinner. *Diss. Absts.,* 1968, 29(4A):1262-A.

Watson, J. D. *The double helix.* New York: Signet Books, 1968.

Wolanski, N. Genetic and ecological factors in human growth. *Human Biol.,* 1970, *42*(3):349-368.